PARENT RESOURCES

To facilitate parent interaction with children as they read *Heroes Just Like You*, WAP Children is pleased to offer a free, downloadable "Parent's Discussion Guide" to aid in having a conversation with your children about what they are reading in this book.

http://pentecostalpublishing.com/heroesdownload

What people are saying about

HEROES JUST LIKE YOU:

"Thank you, Barbara Westberg, for capturing the history of some of our great heroes of the faith. It is so important for our children today to have insight into the lives of these pillars. Barbara Westberg knows how to pull children into the story and make them feel that they can accomplish great things like these giants. There are wonderful nuggets of truth that can be taught while reading each chapter to your children. It is also a great self-read and easy to understand for children of all ages. I highly recommend this book to anyone wanting to help their child know God is great and they too can do great things for God!"

Connie Bernard

"Barbara Westberg's book is an incredible message for this generation, emphasizing the CAP principle: Children, Adversity, and Potential. This book recognizes that the struggles children face could be forming a future of faith for them. It will inspire you to overlook your troubles and focus on the treasure! God has many heroes in the making for His Kingdom!"

Steve L. Cannon
General Sunday School Director
United Pentecostal Church International

"Once again the power of a narrative lifted me out of my life and plunged me into the lives of heroes. Wonderful, powerful heroes—most of them I knew. With many of them I have shared meals and ministry, desires and dreams, heart and history—and it all centered on Jesus Christ. My only question for Barbara Westberg is—'When is volume two coming out?'"

P. D. Buford
Associate Editor of Word Aflame Publications

"I am so thankful that Sis. Westberg has given us this wonderful tool to help us pass down our Apostolic heritage to the next generation. This book is an excellent resource to add to any Sunday school, Christian school, or homeschool curriculum. We have enjoyed sharing and discussing these inspirational stories with our children during our family devotions."

Jaye M. Rodenbush

HEROES JUST LIKE YOU!

BY: BARBARA WESTBERG

WAP CHILDREN
An Imprint of Word Aflame Press

HEROES JUST LIKE YOU

by Barbara Westberg

© 2013 Barbara Westberg
Cover design by Laura Merchant
Interior design by Tim Cummings
Illustrations by Jordana Reeece

The chapter "Dr. M.D. Treece" was written by Betty Treece, wife of Marvin Treece.
© 2013 Betty Treece.
Permission to publish granted by the author

The chapter "Stanley Chambers" was written by Judy Bentley, daughter of S. W. Chambers.
© 2012 Judy Bentley
Permission to publish granted by the author

"Red Hair Is Special"
© 2005 W. C. Parkey
Used by permission

Published by Word Aflame Press, 8855 Dunn Road, Hazelwood, MO 63042.

Printed in the United States of America.

All Scripture quotations in this book are from the King James Version of the Bible unless otherwise identified.

Library of Congress Cataloging-in-Publication Data

Westberg, Barbara.
  Heroes just like you / Barbara Westberg.
     pages cm
  1. Oneness Pentecostal churches--Biography. I. Title.
  BX8763.W43 2013
  289.9'40922--dc23
  [B]
                                        2013025424

CONTENTS

ACKNOWLEDGMENTS

Thank you to . . .

The Pentecostal school teacher whose idea inspired this book. (Sorry I do not have her name, but God knows.)

Robin Johnston, editor in chief of the United Pentecostal Church International, who has graciously taken my calls and given me guidance.

Sharon Jadrnicek; Linda Short; Mary Loudermilk; and my husband, Francis Westberg, for their honest and insightful critiques that kept me rewriting until they nodded their approval.

Betty Treece and Judy Bentley, who have granted permission to include the chapters they wrote.

Jody LaFleur, who graciously granted permission to quote from her father's book, *You Gotta Have the Want To*.

The families of the great men and women covered in this book. Their memories have filled in the blanks and added color to these stories.

"The godly people in the land are my true heroes!
I take pleasure in them!"
(Psalm 16:3, New Living Translation)

INTRODUCTION

A hero? Me? I'm not a hero. I can never be a hero because . . .

I have a disability. So did Allan Oggs. Yet God gave him power to overcome and used him to show others how they too could overcome.

I'm a misfit. Twelve-year-old Benjamin Urshan was a refugee, often without mother or father or a home. Yet he became a great evangelist and pastor.

I'm weak and I'm afraid. Carrie Eastridge felt the same way. Yet God gave her strength to build churches on an Indian reservation and in Africa.

I have been mistreated. So was Marvin Treece. Yet God gave him the determination and the smarts to become a great scholar of God's Word.

I am rejected. Seventeen-year-old Elly Hansen was cast out by her father. Yet she cared for homeless lepers and their rejected children.

I'm just an ordinary guy. Stanley Chambers felt the same way. Yet God chose him to be an extraordinary leader as the general superintendent of the United Pentecostal Church.

I've goofed up. So did T. W. Barnes. Yet God worked through him to heal the sick and minister to the hurting.

I live out in the middle of nowhere and go to a little church. So did W. C. Parkey. Yet God used him to inspire hundreds of people to do great things.

God can take anyone from anywhere and do anything through them. You too can become a hero just like these men and women.

What do you have to do?

Just give God a chance.

ALLAN OGGS, SR.

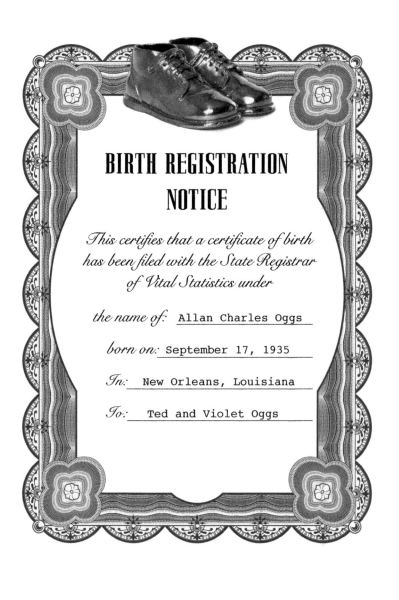

BIRTH REGISTRATION
NOTICE

*This certifies that a certificate of birth
has been filed with the State Registrar
of Vital Statistics under*

the name of: Allan Charles Oggs

born on: September 17, 1935

In: New Orleans, Louisiana

To: Ted and Violet Oggs

THE BOY WHO WANTED TO

At the top of his want list, Allan scribbled, bike. He was the only boy in his class who did not have a bicycle. Oh, how he wanted to ride a bike. Watching his buddies parade by was like sand in his eyes—tough to handle. But nothing had ever been easy for Allan.

When other babies were crawling, Allan was turning over. When other toddlers were walking, he was crawling. When other boys were running, he was stumbling and falling and getting up and trying again. Even though Allan wobbled when he walked, and slurred when he talked, he did not know he was crippled. "Cripple" was a no-no word at the Oggs's house.

"Please, Mom. Dad, I want a bike. All the guys have bikes," Allan begged.

His parents knew that balancing on a bike would be a major challenge for him. But they wanted their son to be as much like the other boys as possible. So one day his dad brought home a bright red bicycle, the most beautiful bike that Allan had ever seen.

That day the Battle of the Bike began.

After several attempts to ride, Allan was red and black and blue—bloody, battered, and bruised. The bike was too. It was a dirty fight.

At the end of the first day, Allan leaned the bike against the porch step. He said in his garbled voice, "You had your day; tomorrow is mine. I'll break you tomorrow. I'll ride you. If I die, right before I die, I'm going to ride you."

The next morning he pushed the bike away from the step and climbed on . . . and fell off. He climbed on again. The wheels rolled a few feet. Allan tumbled. He got up. He was determined to conquer that wild beast.

The battle raged.

His parents watched and held their breath.

Then . . . Allan climbed on and stayed on. Not looking to the right or the left and stiff as a board, he pedaled down the street.

Mother said, "Remember, Ted, when the doctor told us that our baby had cerebral palsy?"

Dad nodded. "Yes, he said that if our son lived, he wouldn't see or walk or talk."

Cerebral palsy is a disorder of muscle movement and coordination. It is caused by an injury to a baby's brain that occurs before birth or during infancy. It affects the part of the brain that controls body movement.

As Allan's parents talked about him, boy and bike disappeared around the corner, wobbling, but upright. They turned to watch the opposite corner, waiting for him to reappear.

Mother smiled through her happy tears, "That doctor did not know our God. Pastor Thomas came to the hospital every day to pray for our baby."

Dad added, "People all over the country prayed."

Mother pointed. "Here he comes now."

They cheered as Allan wobbled by. He grinned, but did not take his eyes off the sidewalk ahead. Around the corner he disappeared again.

As his parents waited for him to ride around the block, his mother sighed, "It has been so hard not doing everything for him."

Allen's dad agreed, "I know, but we can't baby him. We have to let him learn."

"Here he comes again!"

This time around Allan dared to loosen one hand's grip on the handlebars long enough to wave at his cheering parents. Around and around the block the grinning boy went until he ran out of steam.

He parked his bike beside the step and fell off laughing. He pointed at the red beast and said, "I told you I would ride you."

As he walked away, he jerked to a stop, turned around, and asked, "What did you say? If you think I can't do it again, I'll climb right back on and show you."

The Battle of the Bike was over. Allan was the victor!

That was only one of the many battles that Allan fought to do the things that other children did so easily— things like jumping and climbing and writing. Anything that required coordination, even drinking from a glass, was a struggle.

His favorite form of therapy was playing ball with his preacher dad. One big problem was his right arm. It had a mind of its own. He never knew what it was going to do—flop or drop, jerk or shirk.

His dad wound up and pitched. "Here it comes, Son. Catch!"

Allan looked up, slung his arms, wobbled backward, and fell. He got up, stumbled over to the ball, and picked it up. He gave his dad a crooked grin and slung the ball.

Crash! Allan's mouth fell open. The ball had cracked the windshield on their car.

The game went on.

Allan wanted to play sports, so he participated in every school track event, except pole-vaulting. The teachers drew a line on that one. So what if he came in last every time? He was running, and he was having fun.

When the neighborhood boys chose teams for a game, Allan waited on the sideline, hands in his pockets, head down.

"It's your turn to take him," one captain said.

"No," argued the other. "It's your turn."

It was always the same . . . unless Allan's best friend, John Cupit, was playing. John was the best athlete in the neighborhood. The captains knew that if they wanted John, they had to take Allan too. It was a package deal.

As Allan grew, he was no longer content to always be last. He wanted to be the top dog, to lead, to win. But how? Everyone else could run faster, ride longer, answer quicker. All he could do was make people laugh. Oh, no one ever laughed *at* him . . . at least, not that he knew of. But they did laugh *with* him because he was the funniest guy in the class.

When Allan was about twelve, he got into a fight with another boy his age named Fritzi. Allan swung his fist, but his contrary right arm flopped. He swung again. Missed. He could not hit the face in front of him, so he stuck out his chin and dared his opponent, "Hit me."

Fritzi shook his head. "I can't."

18

"Ah-ha! You're scared," Allan taunted him.

"No. I'm not scared. I can't hit you because you're a cripple."

Cripple! The word exploded in Allan's brain like a fourth of July sparkler. He was a cripple. All those "oops" moments, the spilled water, the stumbling, the things that meant nothing to him before, suddenly fell into place. He was shattered.

Tears clouded his steps as he stumbled home. Slamming the bedroom door behind him, he crashed on his bed. *I'm a cripple. I'm a cripple. The girls won't ever like me. I'll never be like the other kids. I'll always be last . . . at everything!*

The door opened, and Allen's mother marched in. She sat down on the edge of the bed.

Allan poured out his fears. "I can't . . . I'm not . . . I'll never!"

His mother did not touch him or shed one tear. Her hard, wise words echoed in Allan's head. "Don't you ever feel sorry for yourself, Allan Charles Oggs! You are blessed. You can walk. You can talk. You can see. You can play ball. You can ride a bike. You can do anything you want to do."

As she left the room, she turned and said, "As long as you live, don't ever forget what I've told you." He never forgot, but he was almost grown before he believed it.

That day was a turning point in Allan's life. The physical problems he had taken for granted became huge mental blocks. While he struggled to adjust to who he was and what he was, he got into all kinds of trouble—drinking, smoking, cussing, shoplifting, even breaking and entering.

19

One evening Allan was looking for a snack in the kitchen when someone knocked on the front door. His dad went to the door.

A policeman stood there. "Are you Ted Oggs, the pastor of the Pentecostal church here in Kenner?"

"Yes, sir. How may I help you?"

"May I come in?" the policeman asked.

"Certainly. Come into the kitchen. Let's have a cup of coffee."

Allan's heart pounded so hard, his shirt quivered. He just knew the policeman was coming for him because of all the trouble he had caused. He wanted to run, but his legs had turned to Jell-O. He held his breath and stared out the kitchen window. *If I don't look at them, maybe they will forget I'm here.*

As the policeman sipped his coffee, he said, "Your son broke into the neighbor's house and stole some of her knick-knacks. She is threatening to file charges against him."

Without moving his head, Allan peeked at this dad. Tears were flowing down his dad's whiskered cheeks. Allan grimaced. His thoughts whirled like a pinwheel. *Slap me. Punch me. But, Dad, please don't cry. I don't want to hurt you. I don't know why I do all that stupid stuff.*

After the policeman left, Dad said, "Son, I will get you out of this one, but never again."

Knowing that his dad was not going to cover for him again scared Allan, but not enough to stop his crime spree. He just determined not to get caught.

Allan's early teen years were tough ones—for him and for his parents.

All that changed one Thursday night the summer before Allan turned sixteen. A man who had been in prison spoke at their church. He made Allan think. *I don't want to spend my life in prison. But I am so confused. God, if You will somehow clear my head, then we will have a deal.*

When the altar call was made, Allan stumbled down the aisle. As he sobbed and repented, God understood every garbled word. The confusion lifted. Allan felt clean. He was free. As he praised God, he began to speak in a language he had not learned. He got up from the altar grinning from ear to ear. Wow! Getting the Holy Ghost was even better than winning the Battle of the Bike.

That night God turned the boy who was headed toward a life in prison toward the pulpit. The boy who wanted to lead started down the right path.

THE MAN WHO GOT TO

Allan returned to school a different kid. His friends in crime avoided him like he had eaten garlic. But Allan had never had trouble making friends. Soon he had gathered a whole new set.

While he had many friends in high school, some aspects of his disability made him self-conscious. As soon as the lunch bell rang, he would grab his brown bag and head for a corner of the school ground. Not once during his four years at Kenner High did he set foot in the cafeteria. He could not carry his food tray from the line to the table, and he refused to ask for help.

When he was a sophomore, he started thinking about the future. "I'd like to be a doctor or a preacher. I can't decide," he told his parents.

His dad chuckled. "Do you know how much it costs to be a doctor?"

Allan had not a clue. He did some research and was shocked. He thought, *It costs a fortune to go to medical school. Maybe I should be a preacher. Bible college is a lot cheaper.*

When he told his dad what he was thinking, his dad said, "That is not a good reason for being a preacher. You'd better pray about it."

About this time Mr. Landry from the state rehabilitation department came to Kenner High. "Allan, because of your disability the state will pay for your education—room, board, and tuition. You can go to any college you choose."

I can be a doctor, after all, Allan thought. *Doctors make a lot more money than preachers.*

The state rehabilitation department provides an education and/or therapy for people with disabilities so they can achieve their potential and support themselves.

But the more Allan prayed, the more he felt God turning him toward the pulpit. The more he talked about preaching, the more people reminded him of all the reasons he could not preach. "You can barely talk. No one could understand you." "You are too unsteady on your feet. What if you fell in front of everyone?" "You? Preach? No way."

Mr. Landry pressured him. "You need to decide which college you want to attend and start the paper work."

Allan went to God. "If You really are calling me to preach, then let me be asked to preach the next youth rally." All the while Allan was thinking, *That's not about to happen. I've never even testified more than a dozen words in my life.*

Ring-ring-ring.

"Oggs's residence. Allan speaking."

"Brother Allan, would you be the speaker at our next youth rally?"

God was erasing all doubt from Allan's mind.

At the youth rally Allan walked to the pulpit and read his text. He felt God's warm hand touch the top of his head and massage him all the way to his toes. Without notes he preached for almost an hour.

At the end of the service, people crowded around to compliment him. But Allan dashed for a Sunday school room and fell on his knees. "Lord, there is so much about You that I don't understand; but if You will occasionally let me feel what I felt tonight in the pulpit, I will preach for You the rest of my life."

Allan's decision was made. "I want to go to the Pentecostal Bible Institute in Tupelo, Mississippi," he told Mr. Landry. "I am going to be a preacher."

Mr. Landry's eyebrows went up. "You? A preacher? But . . . but you can't."

But Allan could and he would. Finally, Mr. Landry threw up his hands. The state of Louisiana would pay for

Allan Oggs, the guy with the herky-jerky walk and the mumbly-jumbly talk, to go to Bible college.

Life in the dorm at PBI was another challenge for Allan.

"I can't shave in front of all those guys," Allan wailed to John Cupit, his roommate.

"Don't worry. I'll bring hot water to our room," his best buddy said.

Buttons were another big problem. Someone had to button the top button of Allan's shirt and tie his tie. Thank God for John.

Another major hurdle was writing. His handwriting looked like Chinese. With his sense of humor, Allan often turned this to his advantage. When he didn't know the answer to a question, he made sure his scribbling was not legible. Often the teacher was embarrassed to ask him to read it and marked it correct.

During the first year of Bible college, Allan realized that if he were willing to pay the price, he could be, not just a good preacher, but a great preacher. He remembered his mother's words, "You can do anything you want to." For once, the guy who wanted to lead believed he could.

At the end of his second year he married Gwenelda Vanderoff.

At the end of his third year when he graduated, Allan and Gwenelda were expecting a baby. They loaded everything they owned in a small trailer and headed for Port Sulphur, Louisiana, to take care of his dad's daughter work. The guy everyone said could not preach was preaching.

The years rolled by as the Oggses pastored, evangelized, and reared three children, Allan Jr., Debra, and Jody. They moved to St. Louis where Brother Oggs worked in the Youth Department of the United Pentecostal Church. He traveled all over the country promoting youth work.

He was a guest speaker on Dr. James Dobson's *Focus on the Family* radio program. People around the world listened in awe to his amazing story.

His highest honor came when he was asked to preach at the general conference of the United Pentecostal Church at Miami, Florida. Everyone in the UPC knew him. They knew how he walked, how he talked. He was accepted. He could relax. Allan Oggs, the guy with the herky-jerky walk and the mumbly-jumbly talk, preached to thousands.

The boy who wanted to had arrived—he was the man who got to.

JUST LIKE YOU

"I can do all things through Christ which strengtheneth me" (Philippians 4:13).

Allan was just like you. He had dreams and he had disabilities. You may have poor coordination or be dyslexic or stutter or (you fill in the blank). Whatever your obstacle, you can overcome it . . . if you want to. Like

25

Allan won the Battle of the Bike and many other battles, you, too, can be a winner. Make up your mind, ask God for help, and do it!

Material for this chapter is condensed from You Gotta Have the Want To *by Allan C. Oggs, Sr. with Sherry Andrews. Permission to use it was granted by Jody LaFleur, daughter of Allan Oggs, Sr.*

BENJAMIN URSHAN

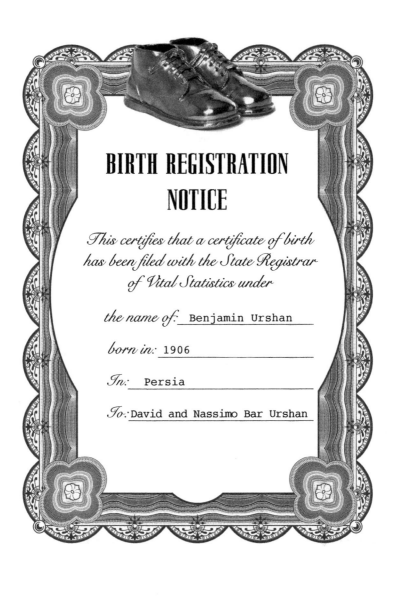

BIRTH REGISTRATION NOTICE

This certifies that a certificate of birth has been filed with the State Registrar of Vital Statistics under

the name of: Benjamin Urshan

born in: 1906

In: Persia

To: David and Nassimo Bar Urshan

THE BOY WHO WAS PERSECUTED

As the youngest of the five Urshan boys, Benjamin was given the lightest chores. He had lots of play time. He spent hours splashing in the bubbling brook flowing in front of his family's roomy two-story brick home. His fingers were often stained purple from the fresh grapes he had picked from their vineyard.

Life in Benjamin's village, Abajaloo in northern Persia, was peaceful . . . until 1914 when everything was thrown into chaos. World War I squeezed its ugly claws around eight-year-old Benjamin's world.

Persia was renamed Iran in 1935.

His father, a respected Presbyterian minister, gathered his wife and sons around him. "The Muslim leaders and the Turks have declared a *jihad*. All Christians are to be killed."

Muslims are followers of Mohammad.

Benjamin's eyes grew wide. "But why?"

Father's shoulders slumped. "Because the Muslim religion teaches its followers to hate everyone who does not worship their god, Allah. We worship Jesus, the one true God. He teaches us to love everyone, even our enemies."

Turks are citizens of Turkey.

A **jihad** is a religious war.

"Then we should tell them about Jesus," Benjamin said.

Father's eyes grew misty. "That is what I have been trying to do." He took a deep breath. "The Muslims have sent for the brutal Kurds. They promised them the possessions of any Christians they kill. We must pray."

Benjamin fell to his knees.

Soon the wild Kurds came storming down the mountain, butchering and plundering. Blood flowed. Benjamin saw horrible things. One Christian was burned alive. Another was dragged behind a horse until he died. Another was skinned alive.

The Kurds were tribes of uncivilized people who lived in the mountains.

But not all Muslims hated the Christians. A kind Muslim neighbor hid the Urshans in his house. After three days he said, "I'm sorry, but you must leave. My family will be killed if you stay here any longer."

Amid the boom of cannons and the bang of guns, the Urshans crept through the weeds to an abandoned building. All day Father, Mother, and their four boys huddled in the filthy, stinking outhouse the size of a small closet.

Benjamin gagged. "I can't breathe. It stinks in here!"

Big brother Timothy whispered, "It is good that Andrew has gone north to preach. There would not be room for him in here."

Mother rubbed her forehead. "I pray that Andrew and the Christians with him are safe."

Four years before Benjamin was born, eighteen-year-old Andrew, the oldest Urshan son, had gone to the

United States to get an education. Benjamin had never met this big brother until the past spring when Andrew had brought his family the good news of the gospel. Everyone in the family, except Father and Benjamin, had been baptized in Jesus' name and received the Holy Ghost.

Father said quietly, "We must pray for Andrew, as I am sure he is praying for us. As soon as it gets dark, we will try to get to the church. Many have gone there for refuge."

Cramped in the stinky outhouse, Benjamin itched all over.

"Stop wiggling," Timothy ordered.

Benjamin sneezed.

"Be quiet," Father murmured.

Benjamin thought night would never come. But it did. Father cracked the door open and peered through the darkness. He whispered, "Follow me. Don't make a sound."

With Father holding one hand and Mother the other, and his big brothers right behind them, Benjamin tiptoed through the black night. The wind felt like Kurds breathing down his neck. The shadows looked like Kurds stalking them. They could not see their enemies, but they felt their evil presence.

Father stopped in front of a stable. "This is as far as we dare go." Slowly he opened the squeaky door.

As the door shut behind them, Mother whispered, "Thank You, Jesus." She turned toward the boys. "Cover up with hay. It will keep you warm."

Little Ben curled up next to his mother under a blanket of hay. It was prickly, but it smelled sweet. Soon he was fast asleep.

For three days and nights, the Urshans hid in the stable.

"Somehow we must get past the Kurds to the church. Surely they will not destroy the house of God." Father peeked out a knothole. "I see two armed Muslims. They are my friends. We can trust them. I will ask them to help us."

Benjamin, with hay sticking all over him, clung to his mother's hand as they followed the kind men across the village.

At the church they joined some two hundred Christians huddled together, praying for their enemies. Benjamin relaxed. For the first time in days he could talk aloud. It felt so good to be safe.

But they were not safe for long.

Someone standing at a window screamed, "Oh, no! What are they doing? Oh, Jesus, help us!"

Benjamin tugged at Timothy's sleeve. "What? What's happening?"

Timothy, who was tall enough to see out the window, shuddered. "They are piling straw and branches around the church. They are going to burn the church down and us with it!"

The prayers grew louder.

A watchman yelled, "They are about to light the fire!"

The prayers grew louder still.

"Wait! Silence! Listen!" the man at the window ordered.

No one said a word or moved a muscle.

"The missionaries are coming!" the watchman called as tears rolled down his dirty cheeks. "They're carrying the American flag."

The Christians held their breath.

The enemy scattered.

"Hallelujah!" The Christians rejoiced. "Praise the Lord!"

Dr. Shedd, the leader of the missionaries, opened the church door. "Follow us. We will take you to the American Presbyterian compound in Urmia where you will be safe."

On the way every time the marching Christians met armed Kurds, Benjamin's knees trembled. But when the Kurds saw the American flag, they froze. Thirteen miles was a long way for a lad with an empty stomach to walk, but Benjamin did not fuss. They were going where they would be safe, really safe . . . he hoped.

The compound, about the size of a city square, was inside the city of Urmia. A high, thick wall surrounded it. Benjamin had never seen so many people in one place. "There must be at least twenty-five thousand people here," Father guessed.

Benjamin held his nose. "It smells like the outhouse."

"That's because there is no sewer," Timothy told him.

"Oh, look!" Benjamin squealed. "There's Andrew." He ran and jumped into his oldest brother's arms.

The Urshans gathered around. "Praise God! We are together again," Mother said. The family hugged and laughed and cried.

A few days later Father told them, "My brother Badal has invited us to move into his house across from the compound. Since Andrew is an American citizen, we can fly the United States flag over the house. The enemy does not dare mess with Americans."

Inside the compound typhus raged. From the roof of Uncle Badal's house, Benjamin watched as every day dead bodies were stacked like wood on a cart and hauled away to be buried.

Typhus is a deadly contagious disease caused by lice and fleas.

Day and night Benjamin's mother, Nassimo, cared for the sick. One day she could not get out of bed. Benjamin brought her cool water to drink and washed her fevered brow. His tears dropped on her bed as she grew weaker day by day.

One morning she went to be with Jesus.

Benjamin grabbed his stomach and curled up on the floor. Sobs shook his thin body. He remembered how his mother's face had glowed when she received the Holy Ghost. He knew she was in a better place, but he needed her so badly. He hurt all over.

On May 2, 1915, Russian soldiers rode into the compound. The Christians were free. The dirty, ragged,

Russia, Britain, and the United States were allies (friends) during World War I. These nations helped the Urshans and other refugees.

hungry refugees spilled into the streets, throwing their hats into the air and shouting for joy. They kissed the hands and feet of their rescuers.

The Urshans gathered their few belongings. As they trudged toward home, they passed burned shells of houses and barns. Would they even have a roof over their heads?

As they rounded a curve, Benjamin shouted, "Look! Look! There's our house!"

Their clothes, food, animals, and everything of value had been stolen. But they had walls and a roof, a garden, and a vineyard. They set to work, cleaning, repairing, and rebuilding their lives.

That winter the Kurds again came on a rampage, torturing and killing. Father buried all of their possessions that he could; then the Urshans fled to Russia. As refugees, they spent a miserable winter in brutal freezing conditions. Often they were forced to beg for food.

A **refugee** is a person who flees for safety to a foreign country in a time of war.

Andrew spent his time preaching the gospel. Benjamin watched as men broke the ice on the river. Andrew led many Russians into the freezing water and baptized them in the name of Jesus.

When word came that the massacre had ended, Andrew took two of his brothers, Joseph and Josephus, to the United States. Father told Timothy and Benjamin, "We will return to our village and our people."

A **massacre** is the murdering of a large number of people.

At home they found the Kurds had once more stolen everything of value that they could find.

"The Kurds may return," Father said. "The next time we will be better prepared." He bought seven donkeys and fed them well. He stored water in goatskins and gathered raisins, figs, nuts, cheese, and bread.

Mother's death had left a big hole in the family. The all-male family missed her cooking, cleaning, and caring for them. In the next two years, Father and Timothy both married. When Timothy and Anna had a baby girl, joy returned to their home. But their happy times were soon interrupted by the fearsome Kurds.

On July 1, 1918, when Benjamin was not quite twelve years old, the wild Kurds came storming down the mountains for the third time. The six Urshans with their seven donkeys joined the long, long line of marching refugees, headed for Hamadan, a safe city where the British army was stationed. The line was so long it took three days for it to pass by.

Horses neighed. Donkeys heehawed. Sheep baaed. People wailed. The dust stirred up by the carts and wagons, people, and animals, burned Benjamin's eyes and clogged his nostrils. Many people had only the clothes on their backs. The aged struggled to keep up. Children screamed as they were separated from their parents. The sun beat down without mercy.

Behind them black smoke filled the sky. The Kurds were burning their town. "Don't look back, Son," Father said. "Look forward. We must trust God. Someday things will be better."

The weary, dirty, frightened people marched on and on and on. Fear stalked them. They never knew when a band of Muslims would attack.

Water was scarce. Four of the Urshans' donkeys died the first three or four days of the march. Soon their food was gone, because they felt sorry for the hungry people around them and shared their food.

Day after day they marched . . . twelve, thirteen, fourteen days. . . . One day Benjamin, walking with his cousin, was separated from his parents. He ran through the mob screaming, "Father! Father! Where are you?" That night he slept beside the road surrounded by sweaty, sick people, but all alone.

The next day he found his family.

When his shoes wore out, he marched barefooted on the hot gravel road. Dust. Heat. Disease. Hunger. Fear. Thirst. The thirst was the worst part.

After twenty-two days of terror, they reached Hamadan. The refugees' feet were burned, swollen, and bleeding. Their throats were parched. Father could barely walk. Ben's stepmother, Narigis, was almost blind. But they praised God because they were safe.

Of the 150,000 refugees, 50,000 were buried in shallow graves along the road. Only one of the Urshans' donkeys had survived. Timothy sold it to buy a loaf of bread for his little daughter. Two days later she died.

Because Timothy spoke English, he got a job as an interpreter for the British army. He was chosen to lead refugees to Iraq, where it was safer. Benjamin's father and stepmother could not go any farther. As they said good-bye to Timothy and his wife, Anna, tears flowed.

Father rented a bare room with some of his few coins. Benjamin ran the errands and cared for his parents.

One morning when Benjamin and his stepmother, Narigis, went to wake his father, they found him cold and lifeless. Benjamin sobbed and screamed, "Father, you can't die! You can't!"

Narigis put her arm around the lad's shoulders and said, "He's gone, Ben. You must help me wash him for burial. We can cry later."

It was the hardest thing Benjamin had ever done.

After they had wrapped his father's body in a sheet, Narigis said, "Ben, go and find some men to bury him."

The men came, carried his father to a horse-drawn wagon, and dumped him in it with other corpses. Benjamin watched it roll out of sight. He felt old and empty.

A few days later Narigis handed him a few coins. "Ben, I have found some friends who will care for me, but they cannot care for you. The rent is paid for two weeks. Surely someone will help you." She hugged him and walked out of the room.

Eleven-year-old Benjamin was alone. His father and mother were dead. His stepmother was gone. Timothy and Anna were on their way to Iraq. Andrew, Josephus, and Joseph were in the United States. He fell on his thin pallet and sobbed himself to sleep.

Soon the money was gone and the rent was due. Benjamin, with only the dirty clothes on his back, joined a gang of five boys who lived on the streets. They dug for food in garbage cans and slept in doorways.

Three or four days later a British soldier took them to an orphanage. Their heads were shaved and their old clothes were burned. Each boy was given a clean white robe. They ate mostly soup and bread. It wasn't home, but it wasn't the streets either.

THE MAN WHO WAS BLESSED

Many miles away friends in England were searching for Benjamin. When Timothy found his little brother in the orphanage, arrangements were made for him to go to England. For eight years Benjamin lived with the Thompsons in their lovely home. They hired a tutor to teach him English and sent him to school. They took him to church, gave him chores to do, and treated him like a son. He was part of a loving family.

When Benjamin was eighteen, the Thompsons helped pay his way to Canada, where he was reunited with Andrew.

Because of the things Benjamin had suffered, his heart had hardened. He had never given his life to Jesus. In Canada the youth in the church were excited and happy. Benjamin was so tired of being sad and lonely. He longed for the joy of the Holy Ghost that the other young people had. His hard, cold heart softened as he wept tears of repentance. The anger and bitterness melted. He was baptized in Jesus' name and received the Holy Ghost.

Then God called him to preach. And what a preacher he was!

While evangelizing in the United States, he met Alice, the girl he married. They pastored several churches in the United States and brought many souls to Jesus. Benjamin and Alice were blessed with three children, Joy, David, and Paul.

From rags unto riches, from begging in the streets to eating at the King's table, from persecuted to blessed, it had been a long road from Persia to the United States, but Jesus had led Benjamin the entire way. The boy who was persecuted became the man who was blessed.

JUST LIKE YOU

"Blessed are ye, when men shall revile you, and persecute you" (Matthew 5:11).

Benjamin and his family suffered much persecution for their faith. But later God greatly blessed him. He in turn blessed many people as he ministered in the United States and Canada. Even if you do not fit in with other kids, even if you have been laughed at or called names for what you believe, you are blessed to live in a country where people are free to worship God. Many Christians in other parts of the world are being persecuted—jailed, beaten, and even killed. Pray for these Christians and thank God for your freedom. You are blessed.

To read more about Benjamin Urshan, order The Survivor, *by Georgia Smelser from the Pentecostal Publishing House at www.pentecostalpublishing.com.*

CARRIE (POWLEDGE) EASTRIDGE

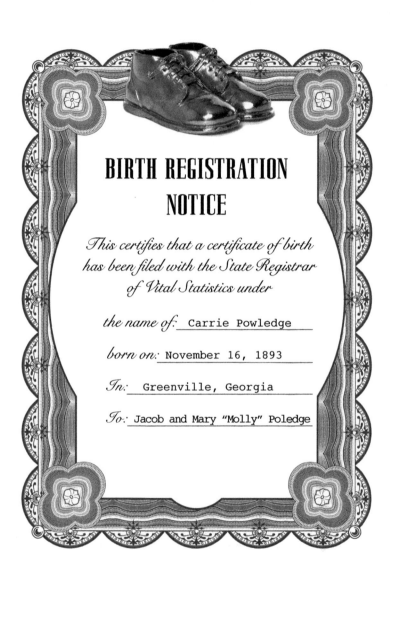

BIRTH REGISTRATION
NOTICE

*This certifies that a certificate of birth
has been filed with the State Registrar
of Vital Statistics under*

the name of: Carrie Powledge

born on: November 16, 1893

In: Greenville, Georgia

To: Jacob and Mary "Molly" Poledge

THE GIRL WHO LIVED IN FEAR

Carrie and Dora watched as their mother, Molly, plodded toward the house. She had been to visit their sister Mattie who lived across the field.

"What's wrong with Mamma?" sixteen-year-old Carrie asked.

Her big sister's eyes clouded. "I don't know. She's getting weaker and weaker."

Carrie ran to open the gate. She took her mother's arm and helped her into the house where Molly dropped into a chair. Dora brought her a dipper of cool well water.

With her apron Molly wiped the sweat from her pale face. The girls barely heard her faint whisper, "Thank you."

As the months passed, Molly grew so weak she could not walk. She lay in bed racked by fever and pain, covered with a flaming red rash. The doctor said she had erysipelas. He could not help her. Carrie and her seven big sisters gently cared for their mother.

At night Carrie tossed and worried. *Is Momma going to die like our little sister?* Pain flooded Carrie every time she remembered Willie Ruth. She died right after they had moved

Erysipelas is a serious infection causing fever, headaches, vomiting, and swelling. Before the discovery of antibiotics, erysipelas was a deadly disease. It is easily cured today.

43

to Arkansas from Georgia. *Had it really been ten years since nine-year-old Willie Ruth died?*

The dogwoods were blooming when Mother took her last breath. Carrie gripped her father's hand as she sobbed beside her mother's grave behind the Methodist church. *Will the pain ever go away?* she wondered.

She shivered as she remembered the horror stories she had read about people being buried alive. *Was Mamma really dead? She looked dead. She wouldn't respond to us. She wasn't breathing. But was she really dead?* Carrie was afraid to ask anyone.

One morning not long after the funeral, her father looked up from his breakfast. "I had a strange dream last night. I thought Molly stood by me and said, 'I'm not dead.'"

Carrie groaned. She felt like a knife had stabbed her heart. *Oh, no! It couldn't be! Could it? They didn't bury her mother alive. Did they?* But she could not talk to anyone about her fears. If she had, they could have helped her accept that without a doubt her mother was dead when she was buried.

After that Carrie started having horrible nightmares. When she tried to eat, food stuck in her throat. The once cheerful girl drooped like a leaking balloon. Everywhere she looked, she saw her mother. To escape her pain and the fear that haunted her, she helped her father with milking, plowing, and planting.

One evening while Carrie was milking, a frisky calf kept nudging her. "Go away, Whitey!" The frustrated girl shoved the calf's wet nose away. But Whitey was determined to get her attention.

44

Suddenly, Carrie's head jerked back. "Eeeek!" she screamed. She dropped the milk bucket. Milk painted the ground white.

Carefully Carrie tried to turn her head. The end of her long, thick, copper-colored braid had disappeared down Whitey's throat. She carefully tugged at her braid. Inch by inch it came up and out of the calf's mouth. Carrie gagged. Her braid was a slimy rope of spit. Yuck!

The next morning Carrie was back in the barn milking. This time she had wrapped her freshly washed braid around her head.

After Mother's death, life on the farm went on. It had to. The girls picked up their mother's chores. Summer was gardening and canning time. Winter was butchering time.

Hogs squealed. Blood squirted. Carrie choked. She hated butchering.

"He's dead," Father said. He took his bloody hands off the huge hog. The dead came to life! The ugly mass of pork jumped to his feet.

"Hold him, Carrie!" Father yelled.

Carrie grabbed the hog's back legs, but that big feller still had a lot of fight in him. He jerked loose, knocking Carrie to the ground.

While the men dove for the hog, the girls gathered around their unconscious sister. "Carrie! Carrie! Are you all right?"

After several minutes, her eyelids fluttered. She groaned.

Carrie's big sisters cared for her the best they could. After several days they thought she was back to normal. She wasn't. Stress and exhaustion often brought on numb spells. For several hours Carrie would lay unable to move or speak. After the numbness passed, she always had a terrible headache. For several days after each spell, Carrie was weak and pale. But as soon as she was able, she picked up her chores.

Little by little the Powledge family's grief softened, and again they joked and laughed. Once more they joined in the community gatherings—gospel singings, school programs, and parties.

At a gospel singing at the New Hope Baptist Church, Carrie first felt God tug at her heart. A small choir sang:

Here am I, O Lord, send me,
Send me forth to toil for thee.
Give to me some word of love
Some word of hope and cheer
And the message I would bear
Life's joys and sunshine share
With the souls who sigh and sorrow there.

                        --Author Unknown

Carrie heard God's gentle voice calling, "Will you be My disciple? Will you go?"

How can I—the baby of my family, living on a farm in Arkansas—go anywhere? How can I take a message of hope and cheer to souls who sorrow? She did not understand, so she did not answer. But she did not forget.

THE WOMAN WHO WALKED BY FAITH

On July 25, 1915, Earl Eastridge drove up to the Powledge house in a buggy. Father loaded Carrie's trunk into the back and kissed his twenty-one-year-old baby girl good-bye. The bride and groom drove to Pastor Waddell's house. They sat in the buggy while the pastor conducted the ceremony. Earl kissed his bride, said "giddy up" to the horses, and Mr. and Mrs. Earl Eastridge rolled down the road.

Carrie did not know it, but from this moment on, she would spend a lot of time rolling down the road.

A year later a baby girl, Bertha Nona, joined the family. The next year a baby boy, Earl Wayne, upped their number to four. Life was good, except for Carrie's numb spells . . . and the nightmares.

One day the doctor called Earl into his office. He named the long list of Carrie's health problems, including a bad heart and a damaged liver. "We have done all we can for her," he said. "I advise that you move west to a drier climate."

"We will move to Canadian, Texas," Earl told Carrie. "Your brother Wyman's family will be company for you and the kids." They sold most of their things and boarded a train for the Texas panhandle.

After three years, Carrie was worse. Often the numb spells put her in bed for as long as three days. Then she would stagger around trying to care for her family. A few hours later she would be down again with a horrible headache.

The children walked on tiptoes and whispered, "Shhh! Mamma's sick. Let's go outside to play."

The screen door banged shut. Carrie screamed as the sound sent daggers through her head. For days she would lay motionless in dark silence. Her medicines no longer helped. The doctors said she had less than six months to live.

As Carrie grew weaker and weaker, her fear of death grew stronger. And the nightmares tormented her. *What if they bury me alive? What if I die like my mother and leave my children? What will happen to them? What will happen to me when I stand before God?* Carrie pulled her fears inside her. She did not talk to anyone about them.

Meanwhile, Bertha and Earl Wayne got away with a lot of pranks. But they also had to do much of their mother's work.

One day the Eastridges' new neighbor, Lelia Brown, looked over the fence. She was shocked to see a little girl bent over a tub of hot water scrubbing clothes.

"Honey, why are you doing the wash?" she asked.

Bertha wiped her nose with the back of her wet hand. "My momma's sick."

"How old are you," Lelia asked.

"Eight," Bertha replied. "My mamma's always sick. Do you want to come in and visit with her?"

Leila did.

Later that evening Bertha climbed on a box in front of the cook stove to fry an egg for Earl Wayne's supper.

Knock! Knock! "Woohoo! It's me." Lelia entered with a pot of stew and a lemon meringue pie. Oh, what a feast! Lelia Brown soon became the Eastridges' best friend.

Lelia invited Carrie to a ladies' prayer meeting. "Please come, Carrie. I know God can heal you. Eleven ladies attend our prayer meeting. Every one of us was sick when we came, and God instantly healed each one. We will do your housework, help you get dressed, and carry you to the prayer meeting."

Carrie nodded. She would go.

What a prayer meeting it was! The power of God swept through that little house. Sally McPherson, the hostess, told how God had healed her instantly. She smiled at Carrie, "I only had weeks to live. But here I am, alive and well."

The ladies gathered around Carrie and prayed in the name of Jesus. A warm tingling moved from Carrie's head to the tip of her toes. Tears flowed. "Something wonderful is happening to me. The pain is gone! I'm healed!" She looked in amazement at her feet. Even the corns were gone!

When Earl came home that evening, Carrie was cooking supper. He frowned. "You're overdoing it. Where are your pills?"

Carrie grinned, "I flushed them down the toilet."

Earl raged. They couldn't afford to buy all that medicine again!

But they did not need to.

Carrie sang as she did the housework, laundry, and cooking. Bertha and Earl Wayne ran, yelled, and played. Not once did their mother scream at them.

49

She spent every spare minute studying her Bible. She was so hungry to know more about God. The more she studied and prayed, the more her faith grew.

On May 13, 1925, Carrie knelt in a corner at a prayer meeting, praising God. Joy bubbled up in her. Words in another language poured from her. Speaking in tongues was a glorious experience. She did not want to stop.

The next month Walter Lyon came to Canadian. For three hours Carrie sat fascinated as he preached on the Oneness of God and baptism in Jesus' name. By the time Brother Lyon finished, Carrie was convinced. "Baptism in the name of Jesus is right. I'm ready to be baptized," she told him.

Every woman in their prayer group, except one, was baptized that day in a pond on the edge of town.

Some days later Carrie realized, "My nightmares are gone! Obeying the gospel has taken away my fear of death!" A deep, strong faith in God had replaced fear. Even death no longer frightened her.

With her new friends and faith, life in Canadian was good . . . for Carrie. But Earl was not happy.

"We're moving across the state line to Durham in Oklahoma," he announced. "I've got a new job." With a sad heart Carrie said good-bye to her church family.

In Durham, she had a vision. She saw a blank picture frame. A brown man's face slowly filled the frame. Then he disappeared, and a black man's face filled the frame. *What does it mean?* she wondered. She fasted and prayed about it.

She felt God tugging at her heart. "God, I know You have called me to do a work for You. Please fill Earl with the Holy Ghost so we can begin our ministry."

But while Carrie was answering "yes" to God's call, Earl was saying "no." Running from God, he went from job to job—saw mill worker, ranch hand, butcher, salesman, and mechanic. And he moved his family from town to town—Wesson, Arkansas; Canadian, Texas; Durham and LaVerne, Oklahoma; Garden City, Kansas—the list was long. Their family grew as five more sons—Joel, Johnny, David, Paul, and Jerry—were born, each in a different town.

With Earl jumping from job to job, money was always scarce. One November when he was working in a town miles away from home, he injured his leg. Medical care took all his money. He could not get home. On Thanksgiving Carrie and the children were alone. They had no food and no money. She gathered the children around her and prayed for food. She ended the prayer, "And please, God, send it by one o'clock. In Jesus' name. Amen."

At exactly one o'clock, a truck stopped in front of their house. A neighbor and her two sons brought in their Thanksgiving dinner.

The lady said, "Sister Carrie, when we sat down to eat, the Lord told me that you didn't have any food. So we divided with you."

Cornbread, turnip greens, and green tomato pickles had never tasted better to Carrie's little family.

When Earl's leg healed, he made enough money to get home. "We've moving to Center," he said.

Carrie sighed. Another move.

After they had been married twenty-four years and moved over seventy times, Earl walked out and did not come back. He left Carrie to raise five sons, between the ages of four and thirteen. (By this time Bertha Nona, their only daughter, was married to Bug Freeman, and Earl Wayne, the oldest son, had died.)

Fear loomed over Carrie. *How can I, a single mother, raise five boys? I have no way to earn a living!* She fell on her knees in prayer. Faith drove back the fear. God had always provided for them. He always would.

By faith Carrie stepped into full-time ministry. She packed the car with boys and their must-have items. They headed to Raymondville, Texas, to a church that had called her for help. Mom and boys arrived tired, hungry, and penniless.

As Sister Eastridge set about cleaning the shabby, unfinished parsonage, the boys ran in shouting. "Look what we found! Paul was kicking a can and this fell out." They held out a shiny fifty-cent piece.

A **parsonage** is a house provided by a church for their pastor.

Paul laughed, "Yeah, and when I looked in the can, I found this." He gave his mother two twenty-dollar bills.

Every time they ran out of food or gasoline or money, God provided for them. Sister Eastridge started churches, revived churches, and ministered to churches. Always God met their needs.

When God directed her to Gallup, New Mexico, to the Navajo Indians, she remembered the brown face in the picture frame. For nine years she preached the gospel to brown faces. She built churches on the Indian reservation and led many people to God.

At the age of sixty-three, she applied to go as a missionary to South Africa to join her daughter and son-in-law, Bug and Bertha Nona Freeman. She was turned down. "You are too old," the board ruled.

Fearlessly Carrie went home, sold her car, and bought a ticket to South Africa. After all those years of walking by faith, fear could not stop her.

In Africa the brown face in the picture frame was replaced by a black one. After many years and hard miles, Carrie (Powledge) Eastridge's vision had been fulfilled. For the next sixteen years she preached to black faces. She built two church buildings and congregations in Africa. When she was seventy-nine, she returned to America.

At eighty-eight Sister Eastridge met death without fear. The wings of faith carried her to Heaven. No more moving. She was home at last.

JUST LIKE YOU

"What time I am afraid, I will put my trust in thee" (Psalm 56:3).

Do you have nightmares? Are you afraid of dying? Just like you, Carrie was too. When she was baptized in Jesus' name and received the Holy Ghost, God took her fear away. And He will do that for you. If you have obeyed the plan of salvation and are still afraid, talk to your parents and your pastor. They will pray with you. God wants to replace your fear with faith.

To learn more about the miracles that God performed for and through Carrie Eastridge, read Shoutin' on the Hills by Nona Freeman, available through the Pentecostal Publishing House. www.pentecostalpublishing.com.

ELLY HANSEN

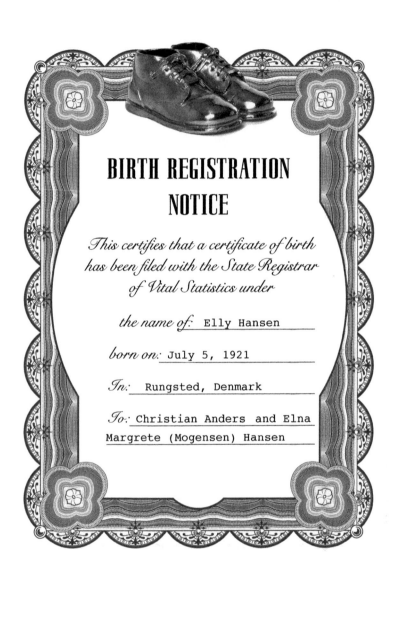

BIRTH REGISTRATION NOTICE

This certifies that a certificate of birth has been filed with the State Registrar of Vital Statistics under

the name of: Elly Hansen

born on: July 5, 1921

In: Rungsted, Denmark

To: Christian Anders and Elna Margrete (Mogensen) Hansen

THE GIRL WITH DANCING FEET

Claps and whistles echoed around the bar. "Who is the girl with the dancing feet?" a hotel guest asked.

"That's Elly, the owner's daughter," the man next to him answered. He handed his glass to the owner, who was tending the bar. "How about a refill, Christian?"

Elly's body swayed with the music, her feet barely touching the floor. The guests' eyes were glued on her; but her pleading eyes were fastened on Christian. *Are you watching me, Father? Am I pleasing you now?*

When Elly was born, her father had stomped out of the hospital. How dare his wife Elna give him a daughter! He wanted a son. Instead his firstborn was a blue-eyed, bald-headed girl.

Three months later as Elna dressed her gurgling baby for her christening, she said, "Soon you will have beautiful curls. Even now I feel some fuzz." She snuggled her baby close and smooched kisses on her soft neck. Elly cooed.

Christening is the ceremony of baptizing a baby by sprinkling him or her.

At the Lutheran church, Elna warned the priest. "Keep a firm hold on baby Elly as she is sprinkled. She wiggles a lot." It was Elly's first trip to church, and her last one for many years.

By the time Elly was three, she ran more than she walked. "Is that child ever still?" Christian grumbled.

His wife smiled. "Not often. I think we should enroll her in gymnastics and dancing. Perhaps that will use up some of her energy."

"Do whatever you want. I don't care." Christian shrugged into his coat and left for work.

Dancing and gymnastics fit Elly like skin on an apple. When she danced, she felt beautiful. When she tumbled, she felt strong.

Elly was the star of the family until her little brother, Mogen, was born. As Christian hugged and patted the baby, Elly's lower lip stuck out. Never in all her seven years had he loved her like that.

One evening as Elly danced and tumbled around the house, her father surprised her with a smile. "Elly, you can dance for the hotel guests. They will love you."

And they did. They called her "the girl with dancing feet."

When Elly was ten years old, one Sunday morning she dressed her noisy little brother. "Shhhh, Mogen, don't wake Mother and Father. They just got home. I'll take you for a walk."

Outside Mogen raced down the sidewalk laughing. "You can't catch me."

Elly chased him. "Mogen, you have to hold my hand."

A plump, smiling lady coming toward them spread her arms. "Stop sign!" she called.

Mogen skidded to a stop. "Good morning, children," she said.

"Good morning, Mrs. Fufk," Elly replied.

"Where are you going?"

"Nowhere special. I'm just keeping Mogen quiet so Father and Mother can sleep."

"Would you like to come to Sunday school with me?" Mrs. Fufk invited.

Elly's heart jumped for joy. "Oh, I would love to." She had often asked her father to take her to church, but he had always growled, "No!"

That morning in a Baptist church Elly heard about a heavenly Father who loved everyone. As she listened, her heart rumbled, just like her empty stomach. She was so hungry to know more about this Father, but she dared not ask her busy, angry father or her silent, worried mother.

The years passed. Two more daughters, Kate and Lizette, were added to the Hansen family. Christian's love for alcohol and gambling grew. Many nights he staggered into the house as the sun rose from its bed. Often Elly lay holding her breath, listening to her mother's soft voice and her father's loud slurred one.

One evening Elna called the children into the living room. When Elly saw her mother's red-rimmed eyes, her stomach quivered. "Children, we are going to move."

"But we like it here," the four children cried.

"Your father. . . ." their mother sniffed. "Your father has given our house . . . I mean he has . . . oh how do I say this?"

"You mean he has lost our house gambling?" Elly guessed.

Elna hid her face in her apron and nodded.

So the Hansens moved. In the next few years they moved two more times because Christian gambled away their homes.

One evening he ordered, "Elly, it is time for you to do more than dance and have fun. You are old enough to work in the bar. You can serve my guests, as well as entertain them."

So Elly became her father's barmaid to make him more money to gamble away. A hard shell formed around her heart. She started smoking.

When she was seventeen, her friend Edith invited her to the Free Gospel Evangelical Church. Elly's heart jumped. *Go to church? Father would never permit it. But I am seventeen. I can go to church. I will go to church.*

At church Elly heard again about the heavenly Father who loved her even though her deeds did not always please Him. "Repent!" the minister urged. Elly looked at the floor. *Repent? Am I sorry for what I have done? Oh, yes!* The shell around her heart cracked.

Late one night she rolled out of bed and fell on her knees. "Jesus, please forgive me. I am so sorry," she sobbed. "Forgive me for being jealous of my little brother and sisters. Forgive me for being angry at my father and for all the bad things I have thought and done. I want to serve You. I love You. I want to be a Christian." When Elly got to her feet, her heart was dancing. Her heavenly Father had accepted her.

The next morning she walked into the kitchen where her father was sitting at the table. She said, "Father, last night I repented and gave my heart to Jesus."

Christian choked. "What! What did you say?" His eyes hardened and his lips tightened.

"Last night I became a Christian," Elly said.

Her father glared at her. "You have always been a Christian. You were born in a Christian nation. All Danes are Christians."

Elly shook her head. "No. It's more than that. I am now a real Christian. I'm not going to work in the bar any more. I've stopped smoking."

Her father jumped up and shook his fist. "Then you are not going to live in my house. You can pack your bags and leave. Now!"

Elly's shoulders slumped. She walked out of the room, leaving her breakfast untouched. Tears clouded her vision as she stumbled up the stairs. Her hands shook so she could hardly fold the few clothes she put in a small suitcase. She sobbed. *My Father does not love me. He never has.* Then she remembered, *But my heavenly Father loves me. He always has and always will.*

As Elly came down the stairs carrying her suitcase, Elna met her. The sobbing girl fell into her mother's arms. "Whatever will you do?" her mother wailed. "Please keep in touch with me. Please!"

Elly sniffed and whispered, "I will. I promise." Without another word, she turned and walked out of her father's house.

At seventeen Elly Hansen was homeless.

As she looked for a place to live, she met her former neighbor, Mrs. Fufk. "It's so good to see you, Elly. How are you?"

Elly dissolved into tears. "Oh, Mrs. Fufk, I-I-I am s-s-sooo. . . ."

The plump lady took Elly into her comfortable arms. "There! There, child! Tell me what is wrong."

"I have given my life to Jesus, and my father has . . . has o-o-ordered me to leave home. I don't know—"

Mrs. Fufk patted Elly's back. "You can live with me while you find a job and decide what to do. Your heavenly Father will take care of you." She smiled, "And I will help Him."

With part of her first paycheck, Elly bought a small brown Bible. She started studying God's Word and attending the Free Gospel Evangelical Church with her friend Edith. The joy of the Lord bubbled in her soul. Her blue eyes sparkled. Finally, her hungry heart was being fed.

One day as Elly was praying, she saw a copper red road winding through a dark green jungle. At the end of the road was a church with a cross on the top. She felt the cry of lost souls tugging at her heart.

"Oh, Father, are You calling me to be a missionary? I will do whatever You want and go wherever You send me."

She enrolled in night school to study nursing. To pay her way she worked during the day. She knew it would be a long hard struggle to become a missionary, but she was determined.

As she trained to care for the sick, the girl with the dancing feet grew into a courageous young woman. Without her parents' support, she learned to trust God to take care of her.

One day her mother called. "Elly, your father is sick. He wants you to come home and be his nurse."

So thirteen years after Elly was cast out by her father, she moved back home to care for him.

Weeks passed.

Christian starting demanding, "Elly, I want you to forget that foolishness about being a missionary. Stay here and take care of your family."

Elly shook her head. "No, Father. I must go where God sends me."

Once again Elly left her father's house and went to work at the hospital. She had to raise money for her ticket to the mission field.

When Elly Hansen was thirty-one years old, a doctor witnessed to her about the baptism of the Holy Ghost. On May 12, 1952, she was filled with this wonderful gift and spoke in other tongues just like they did in Acts 2. She was full of joy from the top of her red head to the tip of her dancing feet.

After fourteen years of preparation, nurse Elly Hansen, filled with the Holy Ghost, was ready to go to Thailand, the land of her calling.

THE WOMAN
WITH THE HELPING HANDS

Aboard the ship, Elly met Martha Perrson, a single Swedish Pentecostal teacher, a little younger than Elly. Martha, too, was headed for Thailand. As the days passed and the ship sailed eastward, Elly and Martha studied and prayed together.

A few weeks later in Thailand, the truck carrying Elly and Martha bumped down a winding road to the mission station. Elly peered out the windshield. She exclaimed, "It's just like I saw in my dream . . . a copper red road winding through a dark green jungle. At the end of the road was a church with a cross on the top." She pointed at the church in front of them. "There it is!" She was exactly where God wanted her.

Word spread quickly that a nurse had come to the mission station. Day and night Elly was called to care for the sick.

Within a year she was put in charge of the crude leprosy clinic, caring for over 1,200 lepers. Every day she and Martha opened the clinic with prayer and a Bible lesson. Ellie did the nursing, and Martha kept the records. At night they collapsed into their beds, often too weary to eat.

Leprosy is a dreaded disease that affects the nerves and numbs the limbs (fingers, toes, and even the nose and ears).

As Nurse Elly patched faces, hands, and feet eaten away by the horrible disease of leprosy, she talked to the outcast lepers about their heavenly Father. "God never rejects His children. He loves you."

One day a man stumbled into the clinic walking on his knees. His legs were gone. Beside him, his pregnant wife quietly twisted the stumps that had once been her hands. "Will you please take care of my wife?" the man begged Elly.

"Of course. That is why I'm here."

After their baby girl was born, the couple disappeared. They knew they could not care for the child, and they knew Elly would. The nurse with the helping hands never rejected a child.

One day some of the lepers came in bringing a little boy. "Look at this beautiful child. We found him outside the colony by a bush." Elly named him Moses and made room for him in her crowded home.

One by one, sometimes two by two, Elly's family of rejects grew. She cared for them until she could find them Christian homes. She gave these children what her father had not given her—acceptance and love.

Long hours of work and unsanitary conditions took their toll on Elly. When she was down to ninety pounds, she went to the doctor in Bangkok. He took X-rays.

"Miss Hansen, you have an advanced case of tuberculosis. You must return to Denmark for medical care, proper food, and rest. You will never return to Thailand."

Before Elly left, her minister friends anointed her with oil in the name of Jesus. She felt something powerful flow through her body.

Tuberculosis affects the lungs and without proper treatment can lead to death.

At the hospital in Denmark, the doctor took forty-eight X-rays and a biopsy. A few days later he walked into Elly's hospital room.

"The doctor in Thailand must have sent the wrong X-rays," he said. "Your lungs are clear. You do not have tuberculosis."

"You have the right X-rays," Elly told him. "God has healed me! I can hardly wait to get back to Thailand."

The doctor smiled, "First you have to rebuild your strength."

While Elly was in Denmark, her friend Boon Mak, the Presbyterian pastor of a large church in Bangkok, traveled to the United States. There he met Billy Cole, a United Pentecostal Church minister. Brother Cole taught Boon Mak about baptism in Jesus' name and the oneness of God.

When Elly returned to her mission field, she realized that Boon Mak had changed. "What has happened to you?" she asked. "You have a power, an anointing, you did not have before."

Boon Mak smiled, "In the United States I was baptized in Jesus' name. I want to share this wonderful truth with you, Elly."

She listened intently as he showed her Scripture after Scripture. "Elly, there is only one God and Jesus is His name. Water baptism must be in His name."

For three years Elly studied this truth. Finally, on April 26, 1965, she was baptized in the name of Jesus in the Gulf of Siam. She came out of the water speaking in tongues. For three days and nights Elly floated in the glory of God.

When word of Elly's baptism reached the Trinitarian mission that had sponsored her, she again faced the hard, stony face of rejection.

"You cannot work here and teach that false doctrine. We will not support you."

"I did not go into this lightly," Elly told the mission board. "I studied baptism in Jesus' name and the oneness of God for three years. It is truth. I can't reject it."

She was forced to give up her work at the clinic and turn in the keys to the mission's house and car. When she left the mission, only the cook, Tauwie, went with her.

Forty-one-year-old Elly was again homeless, but she was not alone. She had a Father who loved her, Tauwie, and many Thai friends.

Taking only her personal possessions, she went to live in the marketplace with the Thais. She continued sharing the gospel and caring for the sick. When God raised to life a dead baby she prayed for, more and more people came to her for prayer. Elly told everyone she met about the wonderful saving name of Jesus. Her heart was full.

Thais are the people of Thailand.

One day a Chinese man came to Elly's small house. "My wife has died giving birth to a child. Will you please take my baby?"

She replied, "I will pray about it. Come back in an hour, and I will give you an answer."

Elly had no regular source of income, but she knew she could give the child loving care. So she agreed to accept it. When the man returned, he was carrying two preemies—twin girls! These girls required lots and lots of special care. She and Tauwie rocked and fed and cared for the crying twins, Amporn and Ampai. Elly often said, "I don't know what I would do without you, Tauwie."

Another day a mother whose husband had been murdered brought her two-week-old baby to Elly. When the baby looked up at her, Elly's heart melted. She could not turn this child away. "I will name him Sandi."

Elly was fifty-two when she was licensed with the United Pentecostal Church. The things that she had lost when she was rejected by the Trinitarian mission board were replaced—a car, a home, appliances, office equipment, and monthly support. She gained a new network of supporters and missionary friends.

She was almost fifty-six when someone left a newborn wrapped in a ragged blanket in her kitchen. He was filthy. A small bottle of water was with him, and a note tied around his wrist saying he had been born May 1. She named him Timothy.

Through the years Elly cared for forty-six rejected children and adopted four.

Until her death on October 11, 1987, in Thailand, Sister Elly Hansen ministered to the sick and led the lost to Jesus Christ. The girl with dancing feet became the woman with helping hands.

JUST LIKE YOU

"When my father and mother forsake me, then the Lord will take me up" (Psalm 27:10).

Elly was just like you. She desired to be loved and accepted, but that did not always happen. Because she knew the pain of her father's rejection, she was able to minister to outcast homeless lepers and their children. Do you know what it feels like to be rejected? Maybe not by your parents, but by other family members or your classmates? If so, you can learn from Elly and use your pain to comfort others. Remember your heavenly Father never rejects His children.

To learn more about the exciting life of Elly Hansen, read Elly *by Elly Hansen and Mary Wallace, published by Word Aflame Press.*

DR. M. D. TREECE

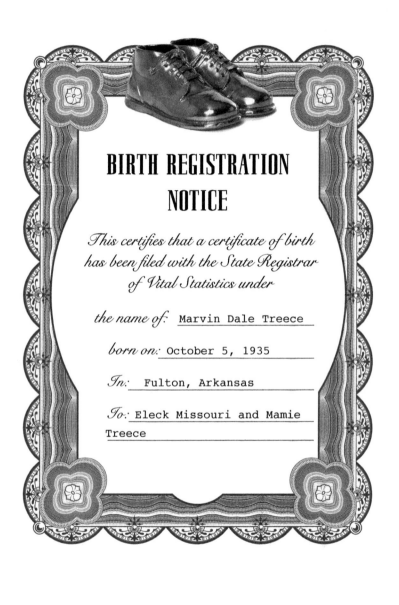

BIRTH REGISTRATION
NOTICE

*This certifies that a certificate of birth
has been filed with the State Registrar
of Vital Statistics under*

the name of: Marvin Dale Treece

born on: October 5, 1935

In: Fulton, Arkansas

To: Eleck Missouri and Mamie
Treece

THE BOY WHO LEARNED TO PRAY

May 1948 in Waco, Texas, was warm and sunny. Marvin and his buddy Barney Mayhand sat on the sun-bleached front porch, singing, playing their guitars, and swapping stories. The music session drifted far into the afternoon. They knew a lot of songs.

Twelve-year-old Marvin and his two older brothers, Herbert and Bill, were regular musicians at local honkytonks and nightclubs. Most weekends Herbert and his friend, a country artist named Willie Nelson, played country and western melodies on that front porch. Sometimes Marvin, Bill, and Barney sat and listened to Herbert and Willie. Sometimes they joined them.

Honkytonk is an old-fashioned name for a bar where alcoholic drinks are served and people dance to music.

When the Treece children were young, their mother, Mamie, taught them chords on the guitar. Many evenings they crowded around her to sing and play. She knew a lot of hymns. It was hard for Mamie to express her feelings, but music connected her and her children in a deep way. Herbert, Bill, Thelma, Leon (who passed away at only fourteen), and Marvin learned to play a wide array of instruments. They loved gospel music.

On the front porch Barney started playing a verse of a popular cowboy song. "Can you play this?" he challenged Marvin.

"Sure!" Marvin replied.

The two played and sang:

They say there will be a great roundup
Where cowboys like doggies will stand. . . .

Every now and then, a warm breeze caught a phrase of the melody and floated it through the air. One tune drifted to the ears of a Pentecostal preacher walking by. He stopped. "Afternoon, boys. That's some mighty fine guitar picking. I would love for you to play your guitars and sing at our revival meeting!"

Barney looked at Marvin. Marvin nodded. It was an opportunity for their music to be heard. The *where* wasn't important. "Thank you, sir! We'd be happy to come."

That night the twelve-year-old boys stood side by side on the platform, strumming their second-hand guitars and singing their favorite gospel numbers.

Not long after that meeting, Pastor Jess Shaw from Crawford, Texas, heard about Marvin. He went to visit. "Marvin, I want you to come to our revival in Crawford. Bring your guitar and sing for us tonight."

Marvin accepted the invitation. He rode his bicycle twenty-seven miles down a gravel road to the revival. During the service he sang with all his heart. Soon he felt God's Spirit tugging on him. He made his way to the altar where he prayed and sought the Lord. Then he went back to his seat.

From her wheelchair Grandma Salters said, "Why are you giving up so soon? Keep praying and God'll give you the Holy Ghost."

So back to the altar Marvin went. He prayed awhile, and then he went back to his seat.

Grandma Salters shook her finger at him. "Son, you're giving up too easy. Get back down there and seek God."

So for the third time that night, May 14, 1948, Marvin went to the altar. This time he received the gift of the Holy Ghost. Joy filled him and bubbled over. He was so happy he whistled. Even the saints thought he was crazy!

"You can't ride your bike home, Marvin," Pastor Shaw said. "You are too drunk on the Spirit. Leave your bike here. We'll drive you home."

They climbed into the Shaw's two-seater car. Sister Shaw drove and Marvin sat on Brother Shaw's lap. All the way home Marvin took spells of talking in tongues and stomping his feet. Brother Shaw kept busy trying to keep his feet out of the way and Marvin on his lap. It was quite a ride!

When they finally arrived at Marvin's house, his mother took one look at his glowing face. "What happened to you?"

Marvin grinned. "I got the Holy Ghost!" Then he walked out the back door to the pasture and had a long prayer meeting. It was his first of many long prayer meetings. Marvin felt God was calling him to preach. But lonely nights and troubled days lay ahead for this twelve-year-old boy. Prayer became the mainstay of his life.

When Marvin was only fourteen months old, his father, Eleck Missouri Treece, had passed away. Eleck, a Baptist minister, traveled between the two churches he pastored. At that time Mamie was a Sunday school teacher. After Marvin's father died, times were hard for Mamie and her five children. The only work she could find was picking cotton on her father-in-law's farm. It was a long hard day's work for little money. So, when Marvin was five, she married Hezzie Horn, a tough man with four boys of his own. Together, Mamie and Hezzie carved out a life for their large family. Every chance Mr. Horn got, he found fault with Marvin, Mamie's baby. This increased after Marvin received the Holy Ghost.

A minister holding a tent revival down the street from the Horns' home invited the young boy to preach in the evening service. Marvin dressed in his very best: blue jeans, t-shirt, and tennis shoes. His message was entitled, "Receive It As a Little Child."

When the service was over, he went to the back to greet his family. Mr. Horn jumped to his feet. His face was bright red. He shook his finger in his stepson's face and gave him an ugly, loud cussing before family, ministry, saints, and visitors. Marvin's face crumpled. Tears rolled down his cheeks. He turned and raced to the altar.

At that altar he found safety. In front of everyone, Marvin poured out his heart to Jesus. "Lord, I found it in the Bible; I've got it here in my heart. They can't take it away from me."

The presence of the Lord covered him. Peace and comfort filled him. Then a thrill ran from the top of his head to his toes. He jumped up, shouted, and danced in the face of the devil, his family, and everyone else. Victory was his. How he needed that victory, for many battles were ahead of him.

Marvin worked from daylight until dark that summer to pay room and board in his own home. At every meal, he was reminded that he was eating *their* food and sitting at *their* table. Finally, his parents told him, "It's time for you to leave."

He was twelve years old and had no place to go. Marvin stepped off that familiar front porch with nothing but faith. His testimony ever after included the Scripture, "For we walk by faith and not by sight" (II Corinthians 5:7).

When two men from the Crawford church, Freddie Waldrop and Charlie Mayhand, heard that the boy was homeless, they said, "You can live with either one of us and work on our farms."

For a year and one-half Marvin lived with one, then the other, of these families. His days were filled with school and work. Every evening he went to the church to pray. In one prayer session, God gave him a special experience and placed a burden on his heart. From this experience and the following days of prayer, a message was born: "Past Feeling" about loving God with all of your heart at all times no matter what a person feels like. (For sixty years he preached that sermon in every revival meeting and each year in his church.)

During his hard teen years, Marvin met the wonderful pastor of the Waco Pentecostal Church, Lonnie J. Hosch. Brother Hosch became Marvin's father figure and his hero. He taught Marvin many practical lessons about life—how to drive a car and even purchase one. He taught him many spiritual lessons. He was Marvin's Bible school and mentor.

Pastor Hosch told Marvin, "If you can be discouraged from preaching the truth, you are not really called." Marvin never forgot those words, and nothing ever discouraged him away from his calling. When it meant walking many lonely miles to a revival meeting, he was called. When it meant sleeping on a hill by the roadside because he couldn't get home, he was called. He never doubted his calling.

For two years Marvin walked by faith, without his family or their support. When he was fourteen, his mother contacted him. "Son, I'm missing you. Come home to see us."

Marvin went. While his relationship with his parents was never easy, it started to heal. He was thankful to be a witness in their lives.

At fourteen he was a full-time evangelist. In the summer of 1949 at the Morgan Camp Meeting, Brother Hosch asked Marvin to preach the Wednesday night youth service. He came ready to preach, dressed in the best he had: khaki pants and a white t-shirt with a fish stenciled on the front.

While sitting on the platform, he noticed the young lady playing the piano. She sang and worshiped, and then sat on the first pew. The young evangelist decided that he would sit next to that smiling brunette. After the service, he discovered that Betty Lee Osborne was sixteen years old. She played the piano and sang at churches and on the local radio station.

For two and one-half years they went to church together, visited, and dated. Finally, Marvin summoned the courage to ask, "Would you like to travel with me and evangelize?"

Betty quickly answered, "I might!"

They were married June 13, 1953.

THE MAN WHO LOVED TO STUDY

The early years of Marvin and Betty's journey were not always easy. When they had time between revivals, they returned to Betty's family's farm. Early in the mornings they went to the field where they picked long rows of cotton. Each full bag meant a little extra money. They did not mind the back-breaking work and long hours. They worked together in the cotton patch and in God's harvest field.

When nineteen-year-old Marvin and his bride went to pastor in Vivian, Louisiana, Brother Hosch told him, "Don't tell them how old you are."

Later the Treeces pastored in Monroe, Louisiana. Each church was a challenge. Over and over Marvin showed great wisdom. He preached. Souls were saved. The young pastor gained knowledge and experience.

Marvin and Betty had a strong marriage, a ministry, and were blessed with two children, Paula Renae and Ricky Dale. One day Marvin called Louisiana District Superintendent C. G. Weeks. Brother Weeks told him, "Hodges Street Pentecostal Church in Lake Charles needs you."

On January 14, 1960, the Treece family moved to Lake Charles to pastor. This church became their home and the foundation for Marvin's ministry. New people attended. God's Spirit moved. The congregation grew.

By 1965 they had outgrown their building. A new church was built, and the church was renamed Apostolic Temple.

Marvin loved the Word of God. When he preached and taught, he passed his love for the Word to the people. The church family of Apostolic Temple loved and respected God's Word.

Marvin labored not only for his church, but for the Pentecostal movement. He organized the Conqueror's Quartet in 1963. This popular men's quartet sang at concerts, camps, and conferences. They also made six albums. The musical training he received at his mother's knee and on the front porch paid off.

He served as the Louisiana youth president from 1962-1968. During that time he started Bible quizzing in the district. At youth camps he played, prayed, and supervised. He was all over the campground, including the ball field.

When the dinner bell clanged, the teen boys dropped their balls, bats, and gloves, and raced for the dining hall. Marvin dashed ahead of them. He collared the boys who had pushed to the head of the line. Pointing to the rear of the line, he smiled, "The first shall be last and the last shall be first!" Groaning and grinning, the boys moved back.

As much as Marvin loved having fun, he loved to study even more. For hours at a time, he sat in his office, digging into Bible texts, and studying prophecy. He began preaching annual prophecy conferences in 1963. His love of prophecy and his desire to understand its depths led him to study the Bible in its original languages—Hebrew and Greek.

80

Word of his Bible knowledge spread. He was often invited to study with biblical scholars.

Prophecy is the study of the future, how God's Word foretells what will happen in the last day.

His hunger for God's Word led him to Cambridge, Oxford, and Trinity University in England. With awe this country boy from Louisiana walked through the stone-arched walkways. With wonder he touched the oldest existing copies of biblical texts. With humility he thanked God for the opportunities he had to study the Word.

As a boy he had walked alone for two miles in the snow to hear Brother S. G. Norris teach on prophecy. With no money, no transportation, and no training, but simply a desire, young Marvin set out on a journey to learn God's Word.

His journey into the Word led him to write the *Literal Word* commentaries: Acts I, Acts II, I Corinthians, Revelation, and Hebrews. He was called to preach at countless camp meetings, youth camps, and general conferences, and he served as executive presbyter of the United Pentecostal Church International.

After preaching his heart at the 2000 United Pentecostal Church International General Conference in Nashville, Tennessee, Marvin stood outside the auditorium. He held his brown-handled briefcase in one hand and his worn, blue Greek New Testament in the other. Looking back toward the auditorium, he spoke prophetically to the friends and family members standing about him, "God just let me give my last message to the general conference."

From that point on, he started turning down invitations to speak at special events. He was constantly in pain from multiple back surgeries.

To speak **prophetically** is to tell about the future under the inspiration of the Holy Ghost.

In 2009, the doctors came into Marvin's room at M. D. Anderson Cancer Center. Their faces were kind, but their words heavy. "It's cancer." After enduring thirty years of back pain, Marvin faced a battle with cancer. Friends and ministers from around the world prayed. His church family, now pastored by his son, R. D. Treece, prayed and believed. Marvin's faith never wavered. He never questioned God.

His last Christmas was in 2010. He sat in his favorite living-room chair, watching his family. As the hours passed, first one and then another coaxed him to go rest.

"No, no, I want to sit here," he said. It was as if he knew this was his last holiday, his last chance to see the family celebrate together. He savored the laughter of the children and grandchildren he loved so much.

On April 14, 2011, at 8:56 AM, Marvin's prayers rose above his gasped breaths and quaking voice. "Our Father, which art in Heaven, hallowed be thy name. Thy kingdom come . . ." His next words were spoken to the Father in Heaven.

In Crawford, Texas, a worn leather notebook was found in the old church pulpit. Thumbing through the pages, the finder read of a revival on May 14, 1948. Printed on a yellowed page were these words: "One little boy received the Holy Ghost." That little boy was Marvin Dale Treece. The boy who learned to pray became the man who loved to study the Word. He had started his walk in faith, and the journey led him home.

JUST LIKE YOU

"He hath said, I will never leave thee, nor forsake thee" (Hebrews 13:5).

Are you lonely? Are you the only young person in your church? Are you the only one in your family living for God? Draw close to Jesus. Talk to Him. Love His Word and study it. You, like Marvin Treece, can become a great leader. Someday you, too, can be a hero of the faith.

STANLEY W. CHAMBERS

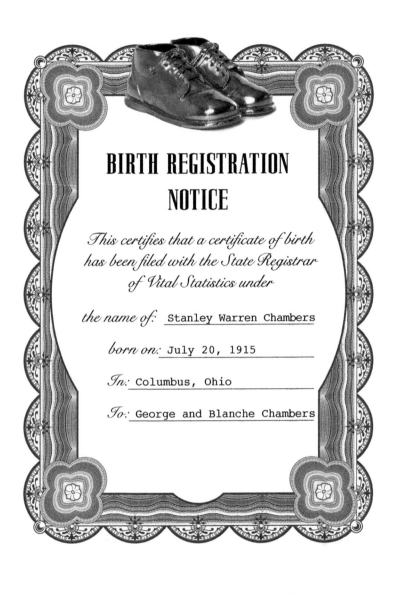

BIRTH REGISTRATION
NOTICE

*This certifies that a certificate of birth
has been filed with the State Registrar
of Vital Statistics under*

the name of: Stanley Warren Chambers

born on: July 20, 1915

In: Columbus, Ohio

To: George and Blanche Chambers

THE BOY WHO FOLLOWED GOD

The miracle of life begins when a seed is planted in good ground. As it is watered, roots begin to grow. In time, that tiny seed can become a tall tree with handsome leaves and fine fruit. How is that possible? It is a miracle from God.

It is like that with people too. When God's Word is planted in the life of a child, great miracles can happen. The child may seem small and useless, but with proper care he can do wonderful things for God.

This story begins with a grandmother who planted a seed in the heart of a kid. Grandma Nichols was a widow with one daughter and four grandchildren. She had a strong will, a sharp tongue, and a hunger for God.

One day she walked into her daughter and son-in-law's house and announced, "I have finally found the right church."

"You've been to a lot of churches," her daughter said. "How do you know this church is the right one?"

"It's a church that preaches the truth just as it is in the Bible. You're going to like this church. In fact, I want the whole family dressed and ready for church this coming Sunday."

"We always go to the movies on Sunday," Stanley protested. He was the oldest child. During the week, there was school. On Saturdays he left the house at 4:00 AM to help his dad deliver bread. Sunday was Stanley's one day to have fun.

"Well things are changing now," Grandma replied. "Be ready on time. The church is in West Columbus; and since we don't have a car, we'll take the trolley." It was an order, and nobody dared to argue with Grandma Nichols.

Stanley Warren Chambers was a quiet boy with a strong mind. He was most unhappy with the idea of going to church instead of the movies. However, he was curious about this church his grandmother was excited about.

Sunday morning found the entire family sitting by Grandma Nichols at the First Apostolic Church of Columbus, Ohio. The music started in full swing. It was lively and enthusiastic. Stanley loved it. He especially liked the church orchestra and the choir. He had never been to a church like this. He listened intently to Pastor Witherspoon's message. He loved the worship and he loved the preaching. The desire to follow Jesus was planted in the heart of this twelve-year-old boy.

From then on, the Chambers family went to church every Sunday morning. Since it was such a long way, they decided to move nearer the church. Stan was happy. Now he could be more involved with the church activities.

He watched as his mother was baptized in Jesus' name and filled with the Holy Ghost. He heard her speak in a heavenly language. It was all new to him, but he was moved by the power of God every time he went to church.

During one service, Pastor Witherspoon announced: "We will begin revival services next Sunday. Everyone make plans to be here every night of the week."

The family was excited about the revival.

One night during that week, George Chambers, the father of this family, had to attend a meeting related to his job. God talked to his heart all during that meeting. As soon as he could, he left and drove straight to the church. In the middle of the service, he entered the sanctuary and headed to the altar. The church people rejoiced as George Chambers gave his life to God. Little did anyone suspect that some day he would pastor this great church.

Not long afterward, Stan went to the altar and gave his life to the Lord. From that night on, Stanley Warren Chambers followed God. He was baptized in Jesus' name, and on February 6, 1930, at the age of fifteen, he was filled with the Holy Ghost. He spoke in a heavenly language as God's Spirit filled him.

When Stan was young, his mother made him take violin lessons. He wasn't happy about these lessons. Like a lot of kids, he didn't like to practice. But his mother paid for the lessons out of her tight budget, and she was determined that he would learn to play. Now that he was active in the First Apostolic Church, he played his violin in the orchestra. All his practicing was paying off.

Stan was blessed by God with a strong voice and a good ear for music. The church choir leader, S. G. Norris, heard his voice and invited him to sing in the choir. Brother Norris told the choir, "Finally, we have a young man in this church who can carry a tune."

The seed was growing strong roots in Stan's life as he become more and more involved in his church. He liked it even better than going to the movies on Sunday. He loved his youth leaders, Brother and Sister Norris. They welcomed the young people into their home, took them on fun trips, and planted God's Word in their hearts.

One summer day Brother Norris took the youth group to the zoo. "Be sure and bring your own sack lunch," he told the young people. "I will provide the drinks."

When it was time to eat, Brother Norris drove up to one of the finest restaurants in town. To everyone's surprise, he instructed them to bring their sack lunches and go inside. When they were seated, the waiter took their orders. Everyone ordered a drink.

"Now you have your drinks, eat your lunches," Brother Norris said. And that's what they did. At first they were embarrassed to eat sack lunches in such a fine restaurant, but then they relaxed and enjoyed their meal.

As they were leaving, the owner came over to their tables. He smiled, "You're a great group of young people. Come back any time."

Brother Norris paid for the drinks as the young people left the restaurant smiling and laughing.

One day the Sunday school director came to Stan and said, "Stanley, I would like you to consider teaching a Sunday school class."

"I'm sorry," he replied, "but I don't feel I'm capable of teaching a class."

"That's why I'm asking you," the director replied. "If you felt capable, I never would have asked you." It was a lesson in humility that Stan always remembered. Humility and honesty became his two favorite character traits. He made them a part of his life.

Meanwhile, there was school. The family moved often and Stan changed schools a lot. But he was a serious student and worked hard to make good grades. His favorite subjects were math, spelling, and all classes related to office management. He learned to type and he learned shorthand. There were no tape, CD, or DVD players at that time, so shorthand was used to record business meetings. It was amazing to Stan later in life to look back and see how his favorite subjects became an important part of his work for God.

Shorthand is a system of speed writing, using symbols for letters, words, and phrases.

Stan was a great lover of sports. He was invited to join one of the school teams. After much prayer, Pastor Witherspoon talked to the young people about school sports. "Your time spent in sports could be a serious distraction from your walk with God," he told the young men. "I'm advising against it."

Although Stan was a bit let down, he followed the advice of his pastor. It was a decision he never regretted.

The 1930s were a time of severe trouble in the United States. Money was short and jobs were scarce. After Stan graduated from high school, his big wish was to get a job doing office work. But there were no jobs open.

Finally, a man from the church, Mark Johnson, came to him with an offer. "I need an assistant to work with me in my electrical shop. I can teach you how to fix radios and small machines. Would you like the job?"

"Yes!" came the eager reply. It was not the work Stan had hoped for, but he needed the job so he took it. He learned a lot about making electrical repairs.

One day Pastor Witherspoon approached Mark Johnson. "The church is growing so much that I think it is time that we purchase a sound system. Do you think you and Stan would be able to install it?"

"Yes," Mark answered. "I think we can do it."

Stan was happy to be a part of installing the church's first sound system.

A certified public accountant (CPA) is a person who holds special qualifications to manage the records of a business.

On the side, he took courses in bookkeeping. His goal was to be a certified public accountant.

THE MAN WHO LED OTHERS

By this time, Stanley Chambers had grown to the height of six foot and two inches. Not only had his body grown, he had grown in his walk with God. He had developed a firm belief in the Word of God and a strong love for Jesus. He was close to his pastor and his church. His hard work in school opened doors for him to do things in life that he never dreamed possible. He was not a show-off or a flashy player. He was just a steady worker. Step by step he followed God. Step by step God prepared him to be a leader.

He chose to live by Ecclesiastes 9:10: "Whatever your hands find to do, do it with all your might." He always did his best at whatever he tried to do.

When he was twenty-four years old, an exciting opportunity came his way. He was invited to become the business manager for a heating-and-cooling company in New York City.

"That's it!" he exclaimed. "Now I can do the work I've always wanted to do."

It was a big step to go from a smaller city to a huge city with no shortage of excitement. He was sad to leave his church family, but he was happy to do the work he had always wanted to do. So, with lots of mixed feelings, he got on the train headed for the big city.

Through his pastor, he had met Paul and Olga Box who lived in New York. When the train pulled into the station, Paul met him with a big smile and a warm hug. He took Stan to the YMCA boarding house and showed him the simple room where he would be living for the next few weeks. As Stan unpacked his suitcase in the dingy little room, he felt a touch of homesickness. But he would have to make the best of things until he could manage to find a better place to live.

Paul and Olga took him to church on Sunday and introduced him to Pastor Andrew Urshan and the church people. Soon he became friends with the pastor's son, Nathaniel. They had something in common. They both played the violin!

The three friends, Paul, Nathan, and Stan formed a church orchestra. Paul played the saxophone, backed up by the two violinists. It was a strange combination; but what they lacked in skill, they made up for in enthusiasm.

Once again those violin lessons paid off. Stan silently thanked his mother for making him practice.

The three young men made lots of memories during those years in New York. One of their favorite stories was about a night when Paul Box led the song service. When Paul stepped back to sit down, he missed his chair. He slid to the floor and sat there red faced and shocked. Nathan and Stan watched from their orchestra seats. They broke into fits of laughter.

"Young men," Pastor Urshan rebuked them, "this is no place for foolishness." Then he turned from the pulpit and saw Paul sitting on the floor laughing. Soon everyone, including Brother Urshan, was laughing.

Two very important events happened while Stanley was in New York City—marriage and ministry.

He met the girl of his dreams, Catherine Strepka. She was pretty, she was smart, she was friendly, and she had been saved since she was seven years old. It didn't take long for Stan to fall in love.

One evening while they were dating, Catherine said, "Stan, I need to ask you something. Do you think God might be calling you to preach?"

He looked stunned, and then he said, "What makes you ask that?"

"I just have a feeling about it," she said.

"That is just what I've been praying about, but I didn't tell anyone else. I asked God to show me if that was what He wanted me to do. Now you have given me my answer. I know God wants me to be a preacher, and I know you are the right wife for me."

Catherine and Stanley married and began their lives together in an apartment in Brooklyn. That was the beginning of their wonderful ministry.

After helping for awhile in the New York church, Stan was asked to pastor a church in Hazleton, Pennsylvania. This new step called for some big changes in their lives.

Stan had trained for office work. His goal had been to be a CPA. But God had a different plan for Stanley Chambers—a much better plan. He resigned from his job. His bosses tried to talk him out of leaving. They offered to pay him a lot more money, but God had spoken.

The boy who had been a follower stepped into the shoes of a leader.

Brother and Sister Chambers followed God's calling to pastor the church in Hazleton. While there, they opened another church in Sunbury. By then, they were the parents of two young girls, Jean and Judy.

Because of his office skills, this young pastor was chosen to be the secretary of the eastern district of the Pentecostal Assemblies of Jesus Christ.

Three years after receiving his preacher's license, Brother Chambers heard about an important meeting to be held in St. Louis, Missouri. Two large Pentecostal groups were considering joining to form one church organization. The Chambers packed their bags and headed for St. Louis.

In St. Louis, they met with Pastor Witherspoon and many other wonderful preachers.

At one business session, Pastor Witherspoon announced, "We need someone to record what happens in these meetings. I am asking Brother Stanley

Chambers to write down everything we decide here. He knows shorthand, so he will be able to do the job I'm sure."

How surprised young Brother Chambers was to be asked to do this important job in such an important meeting. He did what he always did—he gave it his best.

When the final vote was taken, the two groups became one: the United Pentecostal Church. An election was held. Howard Goss was chosen to be the leader of the new group.

It was time to choose a secretary. Who would have the right skills to be the secretary? Someone was needed to manage the office and do the bookkeeping for the organization's finances.

"We have one man here who is qualified for this job," Pastor Oliver Fauss declared. "I suggest that Stanley Chambers should be the secretary of the United Pentecostal Church."

Even though Brother Chambers was only thirty years old and had only been a licensed minister for three years, the ministers agreed that he was the best choice. When the vote was taken, he was elected. Brother and Sister Chambers could hardly believe what was happening. Looking back, they could see how the hand of God had been leading him up to this special moment.

The young family moved to St. Louis. Little did they know that they would spend the rest of their lives there.

Stanley and Catherine Chambers' marriage lasted for sixty-three years until he died at the age of eighty-eight. He completed a very full life. They raised four children, Jean, Judy, Larry, and Jerolyn. He was secretary of the United Pentecostal Church for twenty-three years.

He was then elected to be the superintendent for ten years. Later he was chosen to be the Missouri District Superintendent for ten years. After Brother Chambers thought he was ready to retire at the age of eighty, he and his wife served as missionaries to Austria for a year.

His church work took him all over the world. His work was not easy, but he loved what God had called him to do. It was the miracle of the seed planted in good ground.

Now Stanley Warren Chamber's picture hangs on the wall at the World Evangelism Center in St. Louis as one of the heroes of the church. What did he do that was so great? He followed God.

JUST LIKE YOU

"Thou hast been faithful over a few things, I will make thee ruler over many things" (Matthew 25:23).

Just like you when Stan was young, he had no idea where God was leading him. But step by step he followed God, even when that meant changing his plans. Whatever he was asked to do, he did his best. Because he was faithful and dependable, God promoted him to high places to do great things. Be faithful in little things and God will promote you, too . . . in His time.

T. W. BARNES

BIRTH REGISTRATION NOTICE

This certifies that a certificate of birth has been filed with the State Registrar of Vital Statistics under

the name of: Tom Willis Barnes

born on: July 12, 1913

In: Bradley, Arkansas

To: Lonzo and Margaret Barnes

THE BOY WHO RAN AWAY

Clackety-clack! Clackety-clack! The wheels sang as the train rumbled down the track. A farm boy sat in the box car doorway, swinging his feet. A blur of color whizzed by him. His fingers played with the crotched ruffle on the pillowcase beside him. It held his belongings. Tom was on his way to see the world.

His pockets were empty, but he wasn't worried. His dad had taught him how to work. He could pull weeds, plow the field, and plant seeds. He could milk a cow, cut timber, and stack firewood.

As the train pulled into the station, Tom grabbed his pack and hopped off. The city lights drew him into their embrace. The city throbbed with life. His heart raced as he explored one street and then another. Automobiles sped by so fast it made his head swim. They must have been going twenty miles an hour! At home only the doctor had a car.

From cities to farms, prairies to hills, day after day, week after week, month after month, Tom traveled across the country, riding freight trains, hitchhiking, walking, and enjoying his freedom.

He was his own boss, doing his own thing. Sleeping as late as he wanted . . . when he could find a place to sleep. Eating what he liked . . . when he could afford it. Sometimes he ate dry corn and corn husks; sometimes he didn't eat. He worked when he could find a job. Sometimes he got paid; sometimes he did not.

Occasionally he joined hobos around their campfires. He ate their don't-ask-what's-in-it soup. They shared their tobacco and liquor with him. He laughed at their dirty jokes.

At night he tossed and turned on the ground or in a barn loft or on a borrowed cot. Always too hot or too cold, never comfortable. He longed for the feel of Mom's crisp bed sheets, smelling of fresh air and sunshine. He could almost taste her beans and cornbread.

A memory rolled past his closed eyelids. It was a perfect summer day. Whistling, he walked barefoot through the cool grass and across the creek. Two syrup buckets of spring water swung from his lanky arms.

Tom! Tom!

He stopped. Was someone calling him? He looked right, left, in front, behind. No one. He was alone.

The Voice asked, *What will you be when you grow up?*

God? Was God speaking to a country boy? Yes! He was.

As a teenage runaway Tom stared into the darkness and asked, *What will I be when I grow up? Surely God has better things planned for me than riding the rails and running with hobos.*

More memories wormed their way into his mind.

Mom sat on the porch. He stood by the step, watching the clouds. Something stirred in his soul. "Mom, when I reach the age of twelve, something wonderful is going to happen to me. I will do great things."

And something wonderful had happened. Pentecost had come to Springhill, Louisiana. He had watched as his parents were baptized in Jesus' name and received the Holy Ghost. His folks had always been God-fearing, church-going people. But the Pentecostal message gave them a new joy, a stronger faith, and a deeper relationship with God.

Kneeling at an old chair at a prayer meeting in their home, Tom had given his heart to God. Brother Hubert Wingate had baptized him in Turtle Creek.

Yes, something wonderful did happen when I was twelve. Why, oh why, did I run away? Tom didn't want to answer that question.

Another memory haunted his dreams. He was thirteen. They were in the car; Dad was driving.

"Lonzo, there's a cow!" Mom screamed. Brakes screeched.

Seconds before the crash Tom grabbed four-year-old Ethel and jumped. He carried her to safety and sat her down. "Stay here, Ethel! Don't move."

He ran to the crumpled car. Carefully, he pulled the baby from a mangled seat. Nine-month-old Roland was battered and bleeding . . . and dead.

Before the family's grief had time to heal, ten-year-old Odessa died from an infection.

Tom woke up sobbing. He buried his face in his hands. *God, why did You take Roland and Odessa and spare me? I'm alive for a reason. If I am going to do great things, I'm going to have to change directions.*

No matter how fast the train rolled or how far he traveled, he could not escape his memories. No matter how many people surrounded him, he was alone. Loneliness covered him like a scratchy wool blanket.

One moonless night Tom, along with other hobos, stretched out in a dark, cold box car. The clanking, swaying train tossed him from side to side. Screeeek! The train rumbled to a stop in the middle of nowhere.

"All right, you guys, time to get off!" a brakeman's rough voice pierced the darkness. "The free ride's over. Out! Now!"

Tired, hungry, and thirsty, the homeless gang trudged mile after mile after mile, looking for a barn or a shack—anything with a roof over it. That night as Tom wiped tears and blew his nose, he decided, *This is it! I'm going home. Back to Mom and Dad. Back to God.*

Whooohooo! Another train approached. Too weary to think straight, the homesick boy grabbed the railing of an oil car. He pulled himself up onto the narrow platform. As the wind whipped his hair, his eyelids drooped. *What if I go to sleep and fall off?* He yanked off his belt and tied himself to the rail. Every minute felt like an hour. Finally, the sun peeked over the horizon. The train chugged into a station. Tom hopped off.

He looked around and groaned. He was back where he had started the day before. He was going in circles.

Exhausted, he fell onto the grass and slept.

A few hours later a quivering voice tickled his brain. He forced his eyelids open. An old, black man pushing a wheelbarrow plodded by, singing, "I'm going home with Jesus when He comes."

The words echoed in Tom's head. *I'm going home . . . going home . . . going home.* Tom buried his face in the grass and sobbed. His pockets were empty. His stomach was empty. His heart was empty.

The next train he hopped took him to Springhill—home.

Stinking from not bathing in way-too-long and black from the train smut, Tom trudged down the gravel road toward home. *Will I be welcome? What if . . . ?* He shaded his eyes with his hand. In the distance he saw a man plowing. *Is that Dad? Yes, it's Dad.* Tom's stomach quivered. He stopped at the end of a row and waited.

Will Dad be glad to see me? Will he tell me what a sorry son I am? Will he. . . .

His dad looked up and squinted into the rising sun. On he plowed, closer and closer to Tom. He looked up again. He caught his breath. *My son? Is that my son?*

"Tom? My son!" He opened his arms wide. Tears raced down his weathered cheeks.

"Oh, Tom! My son, my son! You've come home."

Tom ran into his dad's big hug. His hard heart cracked as he felt his father's shaking shoulders. "I'm so sorry, Dad. I'm so sorry."

Dad sniffed. He squeezed Tom's shoulders. "Me, too, Son. Me too." He turned his boy toward the house. "Let's go home. Mom's been praying for this day!"

When Tom walked into the kitchen, Mom gasped. She pulled her oldest boy into her arms, sobbing, "Oh, thank You, Jesus! Thank You, Jesus!"

As Tom's greasy shirt smudged her clean apron, he protested, "I'm dirty, Mom!"

Mom tightened her hold. "Never mind that. You're my son and you're home. Oh, I've missed you so much."

That evening Tom's family gathered around the supper table. To the returned runaway, Mom's cooking had never tasted so good.

Back on the farm, Tom decided it was time to clean up his act. "It was my choice to start smoking and drinking and cussing. Now it's my choice to stop. I can do this by myself." For months he tried, but he couldn't. Sin and the old crowd had a stronger hold on him that he realized.

"Want to go to the revival, Tom?" Phil, his backslid buddy, asked.

Tom shrugged. He wanted to, but he didn't want to.

They went and sat in the back. Tom wiggled and squirmed. He felt like he was sitting on a cactus. Sweat rolled down his back. Inside he was falling apart.

Phil poked him. "I'm leavin', man. Meet you outside."

Tom stayed until after the altar call; then he joined Phil. His friend pointed his finger at him. "Man, God's dealing with you. You'd better go back in there and get in the altar." Tom was shocked! If his backslid friend was telling him to pray, it was time to pray.

Without a word he went back into the church and ran to the altar. "Oh, God, I'm sorry. I'm so sorry." As he wept, he tingled all over, like his whole body was waking up. Words that he had not learned flowed from his lips.

After that night the desire to smoke and drink was gone. His mind was washed clean.

Later Brother Harold Parrott said, "Tom, I would like for you to help me with a brush arbor revival over in the Shiloh community," Tom was ready. He sang and played his guitar and helped people pray through.

During one service Tom looked across the congregation and wow! He saw the prettiest girl he had ever seen. He was smitten. After church he introduced himself. She was Lucille Farrington. Tom's heart dropped when he realized she was not saved. He could not date an unbeliever. But he did not give up hope. He knew that one trip to the altar could make her a believer.

Before he went to bed, he prayed, "God, if she's the girl for me, send her to the altar tomorrow night."

Lucille did not know that Tom and God had an agreement. The next day she worked in the fields as usual, and then walked six miles to the revival. After the preaching, she made her way to the altar. God filled her with the Holy Ghost. Brother Parrott baptized her in Jesus' name. Tom shouted! Every night for the rest of the revival, he took her home in the family's log truck.

Three months later on September 24, 1937, Lucille Farrington and Tom Barnes were married.

THE MAN WHO BELIEVED

Tom had a problem. God was calling him to preach, but he only had one pair of shoes. One shoe sole was split and pinched his foot every step he took. Tom did what he always did when he had a problem. He went to the woods and prayed. "God, if You want me to preach, I need new shoes."

After praying, he limped back to the house. As he walked in the back door, his pastor, J. E. Nolan, came in the front door with something under his arm. Pastor Nolan held a shoe box out to Tom. "God told me to bring these shoes to you."

Tears dripped off Tom's chin. All doubt was erased. He was called to preach.

For the next several years Tom and Lucille evangelized and pastored in the area. Often when they held revivals Tom's sister Ethel and cousin Geniveve joined them.

They held revivals under brush arbors lit by soda bottles filled with kerosene and tomato cans filled with cottonseed oil. Bug swarmed the lights. They sang, preached, prayed in the altar, and gulp!

A **brush arbor** was a rough shelter built out of trees. The tree trunks were used for supports. Branches were laid across the top for a roof. Sides were open.

Yuck! What was that? Tom had swallowed another candle bug, but he kept right on singing and preaching and praying.

When the Pindall, Arkansas, church voted Tom in as their pastor, the young couple, along with little daughter Ruth, packed up their meager possessions—their clothes and an old stove. They boarded a train for Pindall.

As soon as they settled into their new home, Pastor Barnes built an altar on a hilltop. This was his Prayer Place. Daily he climbed the hill to meet with God. He prayed. God listened. God spoke. He listened . . . and obeyed.

One day the young preacher felt a deep burden for the communities around Pindall. "God, so many souls in this area need to hear the gospel. If You will give me a car, I'll go every place I can."

He prayed another thirty minutes or so and then walked down the hill to the church. Two cars were on the parking lot. A man climbed out of one. He dropped a set of keys into Tom's hand. "The Lord told me to give this car to you."

With that car Tom reached fourteen communities. He preached somewhere every week night and four times on Sunday.

After two years in Pindall, God said, *Time for you to resign, Tom.*

Brother Barnes did not argue. "OK, God."

He resigned and waited for God to tell him "what next."

Three months later the church in Minden, Louisiana, called, "Brother Barnes, will you be our pastor?"

God said, *Go.*

The Barnes family of three went.

Again Brother Barnes built an altar in the woods. One day he spent hours praying, "Oh God, heal the sick! Heal the sick tonight!"

God asked, *What are you trying to do? Get me in the notion to heal? I did that before you came on the scene. All I need is someone to believe that I will do what I said.*

Pastor Barnes's prayer changed to praise. "Jesus, I believe. I believe Your Word." After that faith flowed out of him into everything he did and said.

That night a four-year-old child who was born paralyzed received instant healing. Word spread. More and more people came to Brother Barnes for prayer for many needs—healing, deliverance, and direction.

When he prayed in Jesus' name for a deaf and mute twelve-year-old girl, God healed her instantly.

When he prayed for a lady dying with cancer, God healed her.

109

A man fell from a truck, injuring his vocal cords so badly that he could not swallow. Pastor Barnes traveled to the hospital in Dallas to pray for him. After prayer, the man drank a glass of water, then a glass of milk, and then a glass of juice.

No one kept a record of all the people God healed when Tom Barnes prayed for them. Over and over Brother Barnes said, "Tom Barnes didn't do that. God did."

Alisha Lormand was born with terribly deformed legs. The doctors fit her with corrective shoes. Little Alisha hated those shoes and kept pulling them off.

At the Louisiana camp meeting, her parents brought her to Brother Barnes. "The doctors plan to fit her with braces and do surgery when she is stronger," they told him. "Please pray for her. We believe God will heal her."

Brother Barnes prayed a short, but firm, prayer.

Nothing happened.

Alisha's parents decided to quit trying to make her wear the shoes. They would trust God. A week later Alisha stood beside her dad on the church pew. He looked down. His little girl's feet and legs were perfectly straight!

On and on the miracles happened. People came. People called. No matter what time of day or night the calls came, Brother Barnes answered. He prayed. He believed. God answered.

Men and women possessed by the devil were delivered when Brother Barnes prayed for them. Others were given direction for their lives through a word of prophecy. Many obeyed and were saved. Others rejected the word from the Lord and met judgment.

When Tom Barnes was a country boy, walking barefoot through the grass, wading in the creek, God called him by name. *Tom, what will you be when you grow up?*

Tom did not know the answer then, but we know it now. Tom Willis Barnes was called to be God's man.

He believed in God. God believed in him.

JUST LIKE YOU

"Fear not: for I have redeemed thee, I have called thee by thy name; thou art mine" (Isaiah 43:1).

Have you goofed up? Done things that you are ashamed of? Tom did too. But even when he ran away, God kept calling him. God had a plan for that country boy, and He has a plan for you. If you will listen and obey God, you can become God's man or woman.

Material for this chapter is condensed from A Prophet in Our Time *by Nona Freeman and* Pure Faith *by M. D. Gray (grandson of T. W. Barnes). To learn more about the miraculous ministry of T. W. Barnes, order these books and others from www.twbarnes.com or pentecostalpublishing. com.*

W. C. PARKEY

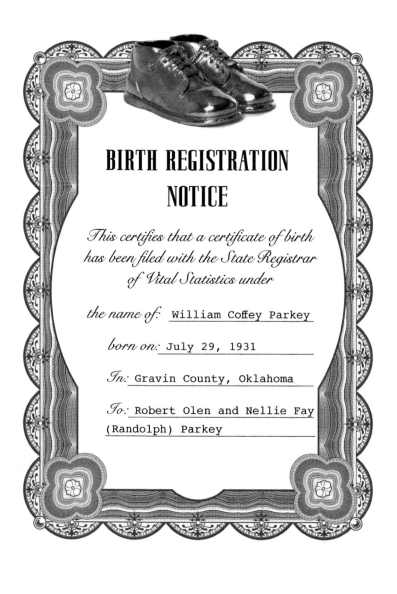

BIRTH REGISTRATION
NOTICE

This certifies that a certificate of birth has been filed with the State Registrar of Vital Statistics under

the name of: William Coffey Parkey

born on: July 29, 1931

In: Gravin County, Oklahoma

To: Robert Olen and Nellie Fay (Randolph) Parkey

THE BOY WHO WAS BULLIED

The red-headed boy shuffled down the gravel road toward home. He grimaced to hold back the tears. He gulped down a sob. It had been a bad day at school—another bad day.

A tear escaped. With the back of his hand, he brushed it away. No one noticed. He was alone . . . as usual. Big brother Bob and his buddies had run off and left him.

The kids' jeers echoed in his head. *Carrot Top. Red. Pinkie. I'd rather be dead, than red on the head. Dead than red on the head . . . red on the head . . . red head.* W. C. sniffed. He would not cry. He might have red hair, but he was not a cry baby.

Arfff! Arfff! A big blurry blob of black fur bounded down the road to meet him. "Here, Pepper! Come here, boy."

The teddy-bear dog ran circles around W. C. The pain in the boy's heart eased. He knelt and wrapped his arms around the dog's neck. "You're my best friend, Pepper. Well, my best friend, other than Jesus." Then he remembered Mom and Dad and his sisters and all the people at church. *Hey, I've got lots of friends.*

W. C. was the little brother, the seventh of eight children. His only brother was four years older than him. Bob was everything his little brother was not—athletic, popular, outgoing, and tough. To Bob, W. C. was a nuisance, a good target for his teasing. "Little sissy! Play your piano. Read your books. I'm going hunting with Dad like a real man."

Dad pulled a living out of the Parkey's sixty-acre farm in central Oklahoma, their mother's Indian allotment. It wasn't much, but it was more than many folks had during the Great Depression. Dad often reminded them that they were blessed to have food on their table; many did not.

Indian allotments were parcels of reservation land given to members of Indian tribes.

W. C.'s toys were homemade and fueled by his imagination. Thread spools were horses, pecans were cattle, a baking powder can was a well, and a thimble was a bucket. He spent hours working on his pretend farm.

Life on the real farm had advantages and disadvantages. Disadvantages included lots of chores—feeding and caring for the animals, planting and tending the garden, and carrying water, just to name a few. Advantages were room to roam, a pond for fishing, and a horse named Pal.

The Great Depression was a time during the 1930s when jobs were scarce and many people were homeless and hungry.

On Pal's back W. C. became a knight in shining armor, a soldier charging into battle, a cowboy rounding up cattle . . . even a maharajah riding an elephant. One day when Pal bucked, W. C.'s imagination quickly hit reality. The maharajah was left sitting on his little boy rump.

W. C.'s dad was a preacher who farmed to support his family. He often held revivals in neighboring communities. He did not take W. C. with him hunting, but he took him when he preached. "Come with me, son. You can be my reader."

At age nine W. C. was baptized. Several months later as he knelt at the altar on a Wednesday night, Pastor Charlie Carter told the congregation. "This boy is going to receive the Holy Ghost tonight." And he did! The joy of the Holy Ghost helped to heal the wounds caused by the big boys' sharp words.

One day ten-year-old W. C. told his fifth-grade teacher, "Mr. Conover, my side hurts."

"Probably just a stomachache," Mr. Conover answered. "You'll be OK. It is about time to go home."

That afternoon W. C. walked home, bent over, clutching his right side. The pain did not go away. Dad sent one of the older kids to the nearest phone to call the pastor. Word spread quickly and the saints came to pray. As they prayed, the presence of the Lord filled the house. The patient got up and danced around the room. Healing did not come as everyone had expected. The pain did not go away until after he had surgery for appendicitis. Yet W. C. worshiped God. He developed a motto he would live by all of his life: worship God whatever.

He was not an athlete or a hunter, but he was a reader. He often stayed up late, reading by the dim and smoky light of a kerosene lamp.

When he was twelve, his married sister Naomi sent him $9.90 to pay for music lessons. W. C. took one lesson. He thought, *I need glasses more than I need music lessons. Mom can teach me to play the piano.*

An optometrist is an eye doctor.

The optometrist told them, "This boy can hardly see. It is going to be a new world for him when he gets glasses." And it was. The trees had leaves. Grass had blades. Faces had features. At school he could read the numbers on the blackboard.

"Well, well, look at Red. He's got four eyes now," one boy taunted.

Another added, "Let's give him a new name since he has new glasses."

"How about 'Four Eyes'?"

"Naw, that's too common for such a brainy guy. How about 'Popeye'?"

The boys roared. "Yeah! Bring on the spinach. Popeye's looking a little scrawny."

The teasing intensified into bullying when W. C. started riding the bus to Paoli High School. The older boys delighted in tormenting the skinny, red-headed, freckle-faced, four-eyed brainy kid. Learning to deal with the ridicule was not easy.

While the bullying hurt, it drove W. C. closer to God. *Jesus was bullied,* he remembered. *He didn't fight back.* Many nights his mother prayed with him. "Son, many important people had red hair—Thomas Jefferson, Christopher Columbus, even King David in the Bible."

W. C.'s eyes twinkled. "And my mom has red hair."

Little by little he learned to brag about his red hair, such as in this poem:

Red Hair Is Special

My hair was in color a bright, fiery red;
That captured your attention if you looked at my head.
I was called *firebush*, and *pinky*, and *brick*;
I was called *Red*, 'til it just made me sick.
I'd rather be dead than be red on the head!
Was one of the things that some people said.
Red-headed woodpecker was what they would call.
Folks thought it was funny; it made me want to bawl.

I developed a complex; I resented my hair.
Down in my heart I said, "This is not fair!"
So I thought the thing through and I then realized
That having red hair was a thing to be prized.
As I learned of the truth, I was happy to find
That someone with red hair was "one of a kind."
There is blond hair, brunette hair, white hair, and brown;
There is lots of gray hair to be seen in the town.

But someone with red hair is not easily found.
You can look a long time and not find them around.
They are special, you see, and you can be proud
With red hair you are someone who stands out in a crowd.
Three percent of the people in the U. S. of A.
Are all who are redheads, I'm happy to say;
The rest are a mixture of colors and kinds.
So count yourself blessed when a redhead you find.

W. C. was not afraid to do the unexpected.

"You're doing what?" A classmate raised his eyebrows.

"Taking typing and shorthand," W. C. repeated.

"You've got to be kidding," his buddy scoffed. "Only girls take typing and shorthand."

"That's not right. One guy takes typing and shorthand." W. C. poked his thumb into his chest. "Me!"

When the teacher of the business class was sick for several weeks, the principal's wife substituted. She knew zero about teaching these subjects. The students were disgusted and decided to strike.

The next day when the substitute walked into the classroom, the girls and W. C. had their heads down on their desks and refused to cooperate.

"If you are going to pray, pray out loud," the principal's wife ordered.

One girl prayed, "Lord, send us a teacher!"

The teacher left the room. By the time she returned with the principal, the students had their heads up. Their tablets, pencils, and books were on their desks.

That evening W. C. confessed to his mother.

"Oh, Son, you owe that teacher an apology," she said.

His shoulders slumped. As usual, his mother was right.

The next day he went to the principal's office and apologized. Word spread. As he walked the halls, many of the strikers mocked, "Chicken!" Being called a chicken by girls was hard to bear. But he knew he had done the right thing.

W. C. was the only one who apologized, and he was the only one who received mercy when judgment, in the form of whippings, was handed out.

120

It was a hard lesson, but a valuable one. *Stand upright no matter who else is bowing to the pressure of the crowd.*

W. C. was fourteen when he told his mother, "God is calling me to preach."

She put her arm around his shoulders. "Be patient, Son. If God is calling you, He will bring it to pass."

As he matured, his determination to excel grew. As usual, he talked to his mother about his goal. "No one in our family has ever gone to college. I'm going to be the first."

She answered, "It costs a lot to go to college, but God will provide."

He studied hard and graduated as valedictorian from the Paoli High School.

"I need to ride the bus to Oklahoma City to apply for the Banning Scholarship at Oklahoma City University," he told his parents.

They gave him money for his ticket and took him to the bus station. Just before the bus arrived, trouble hit.

"Oh, no!" W. C. held up his foot. "Look. The heel just fell off my shoe. I can't go like this."

"Yes you can," Mother said. "You've come this far; you can't stop now. You're going."

So he hobbled around the OCU campus on one heel-less shoe. And it was worth it. He received a four-year full-tuition scholarship!

That fall he packed his few clothes, shined his weathered shoes (one with a new heel), and moved into the dorm at Oklahoma City University.

In June 1950 after his freshman year, W. C. went home—not to the farm, but to a parsonage. His father

121

had answered the call to pastor the United Pentecostal Church in Hennepin, a small community of a few hundred people.

For a year W. C. worked and assisted Theron Chapman in revivals. Then for his sophomore year he transferred to Eastern State College in Ada, where he lived in the dorm. He and Madge Shirley, a member of the Pentecostal church in Elmore City, formed a Bible club with other Pentecostals.

Bill (his college name) often discussed the Bible with his classmates. One evening the discussion became rather heated and loud. The dorm supervisor's wife knocked on the door. When Bill opened the door, he expected to be warned to be quiet. Instead she asked, "Bill, what religion are you?"

As he explained his beliefs, she started to cry. "I'm a backslider from your faith. I'm married to an atheist. Please pray for us."

Later, both she and her husband were converted. Their son, Sim Strickland, became a missionary to Greece. Both of Sim's sons are ministers.

Bill's last two years of college were spent at Oklahoma University in Norman. He worked at the mental institution and stayed in the staff dorm.

On June 6, 1954, Bill (William Coffey) Parkey walked across the stage and received his diploma—a Bachelor of Arts degree. One goal fulfilled. It was time to move on to the next—answering God's call to full-time ministry.

THE MAN WHO WAS CALLED

The calls came.

Brrrnnnggg . . . brrrnnnggg. W. C. picked up the phone. "Brother Parkey, would you come to our town and hold a revival?"

W. C. packed his suitcase and picked up his accordion. Georgia Nell, his youngest sister, packed her suitcase and toted her hatbox. Together they evangelized.

During this time he was elected as the secretary, then the president, of the Oklahoma-Kansas Youth Department of the United Pentecostal Church.

Brrrnnnggg . . . brrrnnnggg. "Brother Parkey, you have been elected as pastor of the Sperry United Pentecostal Church. How soon can you move?"

"Right away." He was ready to settle down.

On September 23, 1961, while pastoring in Sperry, W. C. married Betty Morgans, a beautiful, dedicated young lady. Together they ministered in the church and the Oklahoma district.

Brrrnnnggg . . . brrrnnnggg. "Brother Parkey, would you be interested in moving to St. Louis? We would like for you to be the promotional director for Harvestime radio broadcast."

W. C. and Betty packed up, and with their baby daughter, Beth, moved to Missouri.

A little over a year later, *brrrnnnggg . . . brrrnnnggg.* "Brother Parkey, would you consider pastoring the First United Pentecostal Church in Kansas City?"

123

He would. They moved across the state. In Kansas City, their second daughter, Barbara, was born. Life was full and good. Pastor Parkey prayed, played, sang, wrote, studied, and preached.

One nine-year-old boy in the church, Brad Robinson, reminded Pastor Parkey of himself. Brad came from a family of six children. "I see a lot of potential in Brad," he told Betty.

"You see potential in everyone," Betty responded.

And he did. Pastor Parkey saw in people abilities they did not even know they had. He listened to people. He challenged them. He encouraged them. When necessary, he corrected them.

"Let's get these young people involved in Bible quizzing," he told his church. They did. Brad and his buddies spent hours memorizing Scripture. They traveled to quiz meets. Some they won; some they lost. But most importantly, they hid God's Word in their hearts.

What can I do to help these young people develop their talents? Pastor Parkey wondered. Then he had an idea. He paid for a music teacher to come to the church one day a week. Every young person with a desire to play a musical instrument was given lessons. Brad learned to play a trumpet.

Meanwhile, Brother Parkey dreamed of establishing a national Bible college in Missouri. He prayed about it. He talked to his minister friends. He offered a resolution at the district conference for the Missouri district to start a Bible college. It passed.

Gateway College of Evangelism in St. Louis, Missouri, opened in September 1968.

Brrrnnnggg . . . brrrnnnggg. "Brother Parkey, you have been chosen to be the founding president of Gateway College of Evangelism. We don't have much money. We can't afford a full-time president. Will you accept?"

Of course he would. For two and one-half years, he commuted from Kansas City to St. Louis every week of the school year. Late Sunday night or early Monday morning he flew or drove to St. Louis. Friday evening he returned to Kansas City. Saturday he did visitation. Sunday he preached two sermons and produced a radio broadcast. Then back to St. Louis.

When it became too much, he resigned as president of Gateway. It was time to give his full attention to his family and church.

Brrrnnnggg . . . brrrnnnggg. "Brother Parkey, would you consider moving your family to St. Louis and becoming Gateway's full-time president? No more commuting."

He would and did. The Parkey family, which now included sons William Robert and Bryan Henry, packed up and moved east to St. Louis.

Eighteen-year-old Brad Robinson followed soon after when he enrolled at Gateway. His pastor was now his college president. President Parkey knew Brad was pinched for money, just as he had been when he attended college. So he gave the young man opportunities to work. Brad was only one of the many Gateway students whom President Parkey encouraged and mentored in the next six years.

Brrrnnnggg . . . brrrnnnggg. "Brother Parkey, you have been elected as pastor of the United Pentecostal Church in Poplar Bluff, Missouri. Would you accept?"

He did. In August 1980 the Parkey family moved to southeast Missouri. And guess who followed soon after? Brad Robinson. He was Pastor Parkey's assistant. In Poplar Bluff, W. C. continued to do what he had always done—he played; he sang; he wrote; he preached; he ministered. For the next thirty-one years he gave his life to serving his God, his family, and his church.

His last call came, not on the phone, but when an angel tapped him on the shoulder and said, "You have been called, chosen, and faithful. Come with me. I have a crown for you."

Around the world are men and women whom W. C. Parkey encouraged and mentored. They are sitting at desks writing, standing in pulpits preaching, holding microphones singing, kneeling in closets praying, building up the kingdom of the Lord.

That is how the boy who was bullied became the man whom God called.

JUST LIKE YOU

"I have written unto you, young men, because ye are strong, and the word of God abideth in you, and ye have overcome the wicked one" (I John 2:14).

Are you the kid who is picked on? Do you know how it feels to be bullied? Are you the one who is different? Then, just like W. C. Parkey, you can become the man or woman who makes a difference. Hold up your head. Bend down your knees in prayer. God is calling you to do great things for Him. As you grow closer to Him, He will direct your future.